By Fives to Ninety-five

For Dear Kay —
Enjoy
Rita Holmberg

Rita Holmberg

River Lights Publishing
1098 Main St.
Dubuque, IA 52001

Copyright © Rita Holmberg

All rights reserved including the right of reproduction in whole or in part in any form. No part of this publication may be reproduced or transmitted in any form or by any means without written permission of the author.

Manufactured in the United States of America

ISBN: 978-0-9906740-6-1

Printed in the United States of America

Contents

Author's Note v
Prologue vii

1918–1923 1

1923–1928 5

1928–1933 9

1933–1938 13

1938–1943 17

1943–1948 23

1948–1953 41

1953–1958 45

1958–1963 51

1963–1968 55

1968–1973 65

iv By Fives to Ninety-five

1973–1978 75

1978–1983 81

1983–1988 85

1988–1993 91

1993–1998 97

1998–2003 101

2003–2008 105

2008–2013 111

Merci, Gracias, Danke, Tak, THANK YOU *115*

Author's Note

For over three years now, I've been a resident of the Retirement Center of a Dubuque Health Care facility, located in the hill country of northeast Iowa. History-rich Dubuque overlooks the majestic Mississippi River and provides varied opportunities for a happy, active childhood. The retirement lifestyle, granted, is not the scenario I might have scheduled when growing up here, but one accelerated by age-related macular degeneration, some falls which resulted in broken bones and the reality of MATURING!

After a blessedly brief settling-in period, I found myself aware that I shared a little . . . but only a little of the short-term memory loss reported by many folks. Long-term memory, another story. As I reminisced, the clearest memories were a blend of happy, sad and bittersweet; of the dedicated teachers and generous, close classmates; of the challenging job opportunities I'd been offered; the dedicated mentors and loyal associates; my understanding and loving family. In a flash, the memories seemed to cluster into tidy 5-year segments. This I realized when in the January just past I enjoyed an extended celebration of my 95th birthday. Thank you, God! And, as the college professor under whom I majored in Food and Nutrition would suggest, Thank God for the things we've missed!

Prologue

It's early June and here in the Midwest our late Spring is replaying its stuttering arrival. Sub-zero dawns ushered in cold, snowy days which made us wonder if Winter would ever end. But we knew it did when commencement-time rolled around. Particularly when prime-time TV and the print media allotted significant amounts of time and space to imparting the accrued wisdom of scholars, scientists, and clergy, as well as the ersatz wisdom of "celebrities" and "people in the news." Since commencement addresses are an annual event, pundits are challenged to come up with something original and meaningful. So it was reassuring to learn that a number of speakers have shared my conviction regarding "shoulder-standing." Each in turn with great clarity and sincerity stressed the concept: what you as today's high school or college graduate become in your future can be credited in a large part to the persons on whose shoulders you stood along the way. That is not an original talking point but, in today's "I" and "me" culture, it is undeniably meaningful. As is the corollary: Don't ever neglect to acknowledge that debt nor, at any point in your life or theirs, to consider it paid in full. Express gratitude to those loyal benefactors now and in the years ahead.

1918-1923

"First, I was born," as Charles Dickens began his classic story, David Copperfield. My natal day was January 22, 1918, a typical bitter cold, snowy day, I've been told. Also, typically at that time, it was a home birth. When Papa and Dr. Lindsay came downstairs from the delivery site (Mama and Papa's bedroom) to announce the happy news, listener response was uneven. Especially when Papa issued a gentle "be quiet-behave" order. "Mama is missing you but she needs rest. Maybe tomorrow you can visit her. And you'll get to see your new little sister, Rita Elizabeth." Brothers Loras at 6 and Bill at 4 displayed only fleeting interest. Two year old Helen smiled briefly, then resumed her oatmeal-spooning efforts. Although all had gone well with the delivery, Papa and Aunt Kate seemed troubled. They couldn't help but replay my mother's early reproductive history. Two miscarriages, then a full-term pregnancy resulting in the birth of twins, a girl and a boy, only to have the eagerly-awaited infants die within an hour of birth. As with my birth, in the depth of winter. Would they never be able to have the family they so hoped for?

Our dear Aunt Kate, one of mother's sisters, lived only two doors from our home. She was like a second mother to us. Her children, Don and Catharine, were born in the early 1900s. Rob came along in 1919. He spent more time at our house than at home and was like a fourth brother to us.

As my parents and Aunt Kate knew, God is good. For the next 6 years, at about 2 year intervals, He had blessed the couple with Loras, Bill and Helen. Then, in 1918, me. Before my fifth birthday, our then family of four welcomed John Bernard and, three years later, Mary Monica, to make us a happy and hale half-dozen. The hearts of the

2 By Fives to Ninety-five

grateful, busy parents were giant-economy size, making them naturals in their parenting roles. Their deep love for each other and their respect for all life were clear. Papa was also realistic and, by circumstances, compelled to be a risk-taker. After much thought and prayer he and Mama reached a big decision, to launch a small business that would support their growing family. Whether there's a patron saint of horseradish farmers, I'm unaware. I do have a wisp of remembering Papa talk about a friend of theirs who grew the roots. He home-ground them, as a number of Midwesterners still do today. However, for commercial production quality Missouri roots could be ordered from a firm in down-river St Louis. I have vivid memories of Hohneckers' Trucking unloading the large wooden barrels of roots onto the dock of the small shop Papa had constructed right next to our home. A home built by my Irish immigrant grandparents in 1880.

The location was in the southern part of the growing, bustling little river town. Although called Southern Avenue, the dirt road led to two large sawmills, the railroad yards, the packing plants and the steamboat landings along the Mississippi. Job-seeking immigrants were really encouraged!

Fortunately, monetary investment in sophisticated equipment for product preparation was not required. Our family vehicle, given the age of its young passengers, was a panel truck, so it would serve in the distribution of the 6-oz. jars of Holmberg's Purity Brand Horse-Radish. How that hyphen ever inserted itself into the label's product name is no particular mystery. At that time a great deal of our food was sold in bulk. Any packaged food labeling was straightforward as an arrow: collaboration between a manufacturer and a local printer.

Papa was distribution manager, too. But Mama took charge of the order-taking on the wall-hung phone in an alcove of our dining room. She handled the phone calls herself until she could train each of us kids in succession how to do it and do it well. At a very young age we learned the rules of phone etiquette, how to take grocers' orders AND the serious obligation of getting those orders straight. The phone was an important business tool, not just a toy! But it was fun to take the receiver off the hook and hear the operator's polite, sing-songy "Number please?" Then, after a brief pause, to be connected with your conversational target. Because ours was the only phone in the neighborhood it was accessible to neighbors whenever they needed it. Our number was 3275. When Aunt Kate's family had a phone installed, they were Black 3275, and we became Red 3275.

My father's only paid employee was a neighbor—quiet, kind-hearted Ed Klinkhammer. "Mr. Klinkhammer," always, to us kids. I can still picture Papa and Mr. K sitting opposite each other at an open shop window, a large knee-high wooden tub of thoroughly scrubbed horseradish roots between them. Papa insisted that the well water used, from a pump at the side of our home, gave the roots a unique quality.

Throughout the harsh Midwestern winter, height of the manufacturing season, the two Alaska-garbed root-scrapers worked, plying their razor-sharp knives. They were also fitted with aviator-type goggles in an effort to protect their eyes from the fierce fumes of the roots as they were debrided. Fumes which would sear the orbs of the wisest owl. They were unsuccessful in finding any way to avoid the painful deep cracks and actual cuts in their reddened, chapped hands. Papa was sole operator of the motor-driven rotary grater he had devised. Another eye-burning task. It would be decades later that I learned that it was the <u>grating</u>, instead of <u>grinding</u>, the roots which yielded jewel-like facets that release superior taste quality.

Many times when workloads became too pressing, Papa would have Mr. Klinkhammer stop on his way home from work at the home of another neighbor, Mrs. Smith, and ask her if she'd come to their rescue. Mrs. Smith never refused. She was a widow, with three teenage boys. She cleaned house for some of the town's wealthy people and Papa knew that she could use the money.

1923-1928

My fifth birthday, in January of 1923, meant that I could start school that coming fall! I'd be joining Loras, then 11, Bill, 9, and Helen, 7, in "walking the walk." That was no figure of speech, either—St. Raphael's was almost a mile from home, and everybody went home for dinner at noon. That back-and-forthing, or forth-and-backing, added up! To ease the rigor of the trek, we made frequent stops at a stucco-faced candy shop close to school. It looked like pictures of thatch-roof cottages in an Irish calendar hanging in our kitchen. A floor-length chintz curtain, complete with a bell to signal the arrival of customers, separated the shop from the living quarters of the elderly proprietor, Mrs. Collins, who ran the shop. She had a young foster daughter, Rosella, and a really uppity cat, Methuselah. A glass-fronted wooden counter extended the depth of the shop. It held neatly arranged trays of Walnettos, miniature pans of caramel "tea buns", sugared spearmint green leaves, red and black jaw-breakers, and chocolate stars. What an array! When we would have frequent moments of indecision about how to allocate our pennies, an impatient fixed stare from Mrs. Collins over her pince-nez glasses sped up the transaction. On we marched to school, clutching our bright-colored striped paper bags of assorted sugarplums.

Saint Raphael's was built in the early 1890s of friendly red brick and with warm wheat color trim. It was set close to Kelly's Bluff, an ancient lead-mining site, and only a few blocks away from the north-south-running Mississippi River at the East.

Papa loved to tell us about his own connection with the building of St. Raphael's. When he was about 17, he was hired as a "helping hand" to the men who were the builders. He was proud to be working

6 By Fives to Ninety-five

on the front entrance with them. Especially when the day came to install a long, heavy part called the "name-plate." The workmen hoisted the part up over the entry of the school and eased it temporarily into a waiting open space. But they saw right away that it was not in balance. One of the workmen spotted a discarded newspaper and thrust it into Papa's hands, then showed him how to fold it into a firm, flat rectangle. The "flat" was then tucked under one end of the name-plate and after some gentle pushing and smoothening, it "did the trick," as Papa always put it.

(When I was older and already going into third grade, I could understand why they wouldn't want a school named for a saint who was out of balance, would they?)

Our school was sometimes referred to as "the Sisters' School" because the teachers were all Catholic Sisters. They lived in a nice convent facing south on Emmet Street. The convent also served as a school before St. Raphael's would be built. The young teachers taught small groups as well as individual children of the immigrants. Named "St. Mary's Convent," it would soon be bordered on the West side by St. Mary's Street. My Aunt Kate and Mama went to classes there when they were little. Both loved to tell us stories of those days. Aunt Kate, born in 1879, wrote a lovely little booklet about her life. We'd often ask her to repeat the tale about her "shepherdess" days.

> "I remember being absent from school for several weeks each Spring on account of our geese and their little goslings, which had to be driven, each morning, down the road to a large patch of clover and grass. I guarded them all day, taking my lunch with me, wearing my sun-bonnet and carrying a big umbrella. (This last mentioned being used mostly in warding off stray dogs that might frighten or disturb my charges.) Imagine my surprise, when returning to school, to see my picture on the blackboard—my geese and goslings, my sunbonnet, umbrella and bare feet—drawn by my teacher, Sister Mary Johanna, who was a real artist. She hadn't missed one thing in that picture."

The Sisters were members of a religious order, the "Sisters of Charity of the Blessed Virgin Mary." Often that name was shortened to "the BVM's." They wore long, black serge "habits" with full pleated and belted skirts, topped with full "mantles" which had a stiff white collar. Their heads were covered with box-like headpieces which left only the face exposed. (We all wondered if they still had any hair!)

Sister Mary Albia was my first-grade teacher and taught us about the alphabet and words and printing. And we learned about drawing and paper art. There were a lot of girls and boys in our class. I think Mama said 45 or 46. My best friends were Millie and R.J. Their real names were Mildred and Robert Joseph. But our school didn't use nicknames. They always called you by your real first name, like "Robert" and "Mildred," the names you received at Baptism.

In second grade, in Sister Mary Honor's class, we had gotten our own "First Reader." It was such a good feeling when Papa wrote my name in the front of the book, with September 8, 1924 under it. I hoped that before long I could write as nice as Papa did. Mama said I was doing well though.

My cousin, Catharine, Aunt Kate's daughter, was 13 and went to the library real often. She took me with her one day. We went into the children's section and she helped me get my very own card. I had to sign my whole name, "Rita Elizabeth Holmberg," and my age, 6. The nice lady at the desk explained how the Children's section was arranged. Then she and Catharine helped me pick out books; two for John, two for me and one for Mary. It was just a picture book, of course.

Even before I got my own library card, I'd been to Saturday morning Story Hour lots of times. The Corbetts lived next door to us and Aunt Kate next to them. Catharine would sometimes take Helen and Marcella Corbett when we were little. And before long Helen and Marcella, both 9, were considered old enough to be reliable troop leaders. By that time our story hour fans included my little sister Mary, Stella Corbett and her twin sisters, Jane and Martha. We took our school route and then went eight blocks further on, up to the Bluff-side library entrance, a narrow enclosed stairway leading to the first floor. A big, big doughnut-shaped main desk, where the library ladies worked was to the right and tall, dark stacks of books in the background. So many that they almost reached the ceiling. There was such a nice smell in the library. Somebody said it was probably from the rubber cement they used. I didn't know. And the ceiling was cut out above the desk so that daylight streamed down from two floors above. It made you want to be a librarian when you grew up.

The Story Hour Room was on the second floor. It was very pretty. Dark green velvety carpeting, with beautiful deep pinkish flowers scattered on it. The Story Reader sat on a kind of open bench-chair with curved arms and we sat around her on the floor. The chair was like the ones they had in the photographer's studio when we had a picture of the four of us taken. That was before John and Mary were born. The stories were so good—and so was the Reader. We hated to have it all end. We remembered to say "thank you" to her. Then we'd go back to the Main desk and whisper to the tall red-haired lady in charge: "May we please have the key to the Ladies' Room?" Whether or not we had to use the restroom, it was such fun to go up and down the curved marble stairs, with the dark twisted iron rail. After we returned the key, we'd go out the main entrance on Eleventh Street. Those cement stairs seemed about a mile wide. They were wonderful for skipping down!

1928-1933

Sister Mary Jane de Chantal, our fifth-grade teacher, had taught my two brothers and my sister. The only teacher I'd had so far who did not call me "He-Rita," Helen coming to their minds right away. I was beginning to think that "He-Rita" was my Baptismal name! Sister Jane loved to read to us. Often our Midwest winters forced us to carry our lunch to school and to eat in a damp, dim-lit basement room. It was across the hall from the St. Vincent de Paul room, where second-hand clothes filled long tables or were packed on clothes racks, ready for distribution to the needy. We didn't linger over lunch. We knew that Sister Mary Jane would take over as our enthusiastic reader as soon as she got us back to the classroom and settled down. She sometimes treated each of us to a big juicy orange, aware that more than a few of the kids may not get one very often. She started reading while we peeled and ate the oranges. Pretty soon the sweet, spicy aroma of citrus filled the room.

Sister had already read us Tom Playfair, Rebecca of Sunnybrook Farm, The Five Little Peppers and one of the Horatio Alger books. Lunch hour went fast and then it was back to the regular schedule.

Usually we had English right after lunch. We were going to write something about the wonderful picnic our class had at Cascade Crossing the week before. We had walked all the way out there—and back!—from school to the Crossing near the big gray stone Wartburg Seminary. Papa said this was probably almost three miles. Sister told us we could write a composition, a newspaper report or even a poem. She was going to send them to our Archdiocesan paper, The WITNESS. So we did. And guess what? My poem was published, along with a nice composition by Isabel and a news article by my friend

M.J.—Michael John. We were each awarded a nice, brand-new book as a prize. Mine was An Old-Fashioned Girl by Louisa Mae Alcott. It had five full page color pictures and almost twice as many drawings. I just love it! Would you like to read a couple of stanzas of "Our Picnic?"

Our Picnic

One bright, sunny day
When all was so gay
We went on the picnic
We'd planned yesterday.
Lugging, tugging and hiking went we.
We soon reached the Crossroads,
All in high glee.

(I hope you liked it . . .)

Some winter days, of course, school was called off. Soft, puffy snow blanketing Dubuque's numerous hills and slopes made us sledders happy. But if ice or sleet was mixed in with those swirling flakes, walkways and roadways became hazardous. But not too hazardous for Loras or Bill to take a bucket of hot vegetable soup up the street to the Mahoneys. Jack Mahoney worked for the city. He had a club foot and his elderly sister, Alice, was blind. Mama also sent along some of the cinnamon rolls she had just taken out of the oven.

I loved Arithmetic, too. At school we used workbooks and got homework assignments based on them. Right after supper and the dishes were done, Helen, John and I pulled chairs up to the big kitchen table. Helen was in seventh grade and really good at Arithmetic. She helped me and John if we got stuck. Papa would go back to the shop after supper to wind things up and do chores like bringing in a couple of scuttles of coal and some firewood, before he locked up. The he would join us at the table. He made everything so clear that he could write a workbook himself, I believed! I knew for sure that he made homework fun. When we were almost finished, Mama would put a big bowl of shiny red apples in the center of the table for us. Mary, then 4, and ready for bed, was waiting for Papa to do his "snake trick" for her. She stood at his side as he whipped out his bone-handled pocket-knife and watched him, wide-eyed. He'd start at the apple's stem end and put the tip of the blade under the skin. Then he would slowly and carefully cut, round and round the apple, without one single break in the peel, turning it into a bright red snake! Mary would be delighted and giggling as Papa carried her upstairs to bed.

I started helping Papa in his shop. He made the paste to use on his horseradish labels. (I think it was out of flour or corn starch mixed with water and then cooked. When it was thick and cooled it was ready to brush on the back of the labels and place them on the prepared jars.) I had to be sure that they were all smack in the center of the jar—and not pasted on crooked. I'd line the jars in several rows of 12 each and label them a row at a time, because the home-made paste got thick and maybe even a little lumpy. But the job went fast. Papa paid me a penny a dozen and always added a bonus. Some of it went into the "Bank Day" account we had at school and some, of course, to Mrs. Collins' Candy Shop on the way to school.

That summer a new family, the Breitbachs, moved into a home about a block and a half from ours, close to Jack and Alice Mahoney's home. There were four boys and only one girl, Mary Margaret. She was 13. I wouldn't be 13 until January but we soon became best friends. We would be graduating from 8th grade at St. Raphael's the following year. She'd be going to Washington Junior High School, she told me.

Mary Margaret was a much better baseball player than I was. And two of her brothers, Bill and Rob, were extra good. We had enough kids in the neighborhood to easily make up two teams. So there were a lot of ball games on our street. My sister Helen and Jack Corbett, our next-door neighbor, were always team captains. When it came to choosing sides, Helen never picked me. Then, when Jack needed his ninth player, as a last resort, he'd turn in my direction: "OK, I'll take Rita." Jack, you see, was born on January 21, 1918, the very day before me, and we were real buddies.

We were lucky to have a handy swimming spot in the neighborhood, too, only a couple of blocks from where we lived. Third Slough was one of three back-waters from the Mississippi. (With great creativity we called them First, Second and Third sloughs.) Bright green bushes lined the sandy slope leading down from ground level to the water. The other side: a rocky—and in spots, "coal-y"—slope descended from railroad tracks, used by open-to-the-sky boxcars carrying coal into town. Not the most scenic beach in the world, but we swam and fished in the then-unpolluted slough as though it were like a beach in a travel folder.

Mama and Papa were concerned about safety, so they wrote a request to the City for a part-time lifeguard and asked other parents to sign it. Mama presented the letter to the City Council and it passed. Newt Wimmer, probably in his late teens, got the job. He was posted for a good number of hours a day, to protect us all, from fearless paddlers to older youngsters yearning to ride the imaginary surf. Our parents were pleased at how well he handled his responsibility. The kids liked and respected him. They never questioned any of his "calls."

In between ball games, swimming, a sewing club we had started, and activities at the Franklin School Summer Playground, half a block down from St. Raphael's, our days were full. I graduated from eighth grade and, just a year later, from ninth grade at Washington Junior High, with Mary Margaret.

1933-1938

I knew that I'd keep all my friends from St. Raphael's forever and ever. And before I knew it I'd made a lot of new friends at Washington and then Senior. In high school six of us decided to form a club. But we couldn't come up with an idea of what we'd undertake: Bunco? cards? sewing? At a potluck supper at my house one crisp Fall evening we were oohing and aahing over Lora Kaufman's mother's Sea-shell Green Grape Salad and my mother's Ham Loaf. Like lightning, the notion of a Potluck Supper Club struck. And stuck through graduation in 1935 and a bit after. No <u>officers,</u> no agenda, no dues. Just meet-and-eat, and celebrate our friendship. Dorothy Berwanger's brother, Jay, was the noted football star at the University of Chicago at that time, often hailed as "a one-man football team." Dorothy was an enthusiastic potlucker and a good friend of mine. When Jay was picked to play in the 1936 All-Star Game in Soldier Field, the Berwangers invited me to accompany the family into Chicago by Zephyr and stay with some of the family's relatives. So limited was my travel experience at this point in my life that the prospect of a trip to Chicago was like winning a rocket trip to Mars. My understanding of football was even less than limited. But what a heady experience it turned out to be! I sat with the Berwangers in a spectacular box on the 50-yard line of Soldier Field. We were spotlighted before the game began and all of us introduced over a blaring loudspeaker. Happily the All-Stars were winners, as Jay continued to be throughout his life. Winner of the first Heisman Trophy, he also was widely respected for his ability to handle his fame and recognized his teachers, mentors, and loyal teammates as supporters along his way.

14 By Fives to Ninety-five

At this point in time, our country had been struggling through the Great Depression. Disasters like the stock market crash of 1929, numerous bank failures, unrelenting droughts such as the Oklahoma Dust Bowl, dismal unemployment reports which resulted in near crisis food and housing costs. Bread lines, soup kitchens, and food rationing. "Hoovervilles," springing up in various sections of towns. Harsh realities which our high school classes in Economics and Social Problems helped us young uninitiates understand—to a degree.

I wouldn't be going on to college right away, so I had taken commercial subjects: shorthand, typing and office practice, in addition to algebra, English and French literature, speech and home economics. In my last two years at Senior High, I worked part-time in the office of the principal, Mr. Ralph W. Johnson, and his assistant, Miss Staudacher. I learned so much from them.

Loras and Helen both attended Dubuque colleges. He went to Columbia, a Catholic men's school, and she, to Clarke, a Catholic private college for women. After high school, Bill had been fortunate to find work as a clerk at Healey's Hardware and was still living at home.

After my graduation in June of 1935, the job search had begun. It ended in October when I was offered a stenographer's job in the general office of the National Refining Company, whose "EN-AR-CO Boy With A Slate" dotted the Midwest landscape. The office force was about 35-ish, 40-ish, a few perhaps older. I think they looked upon this 17-year-old as a newly hatched bird. Indeed, for the first few days, I'd have been more at ease if I'd never left the shell. But they were supportive and understanding, ready to share their know-how and skills.

The sales manager, Carl Danglemeyer, one of the 40-ish (or more) age group, was in and out of the office so I didn't get to know him very well. I did know that his two "mature" sisters had opened a dress shop, "La Parisienne", on Main Street next to Stampfer's Department Store. When co-workers Jo Reidy and Gladys Cahill asked if I'd like to visit the shop with them, I was quick to accept. And I was quick to succumb to the charm of the French décor and dresses, coats and suits displayed so beautifully. There was jewelry, too, and a selection of hats, scarves and gloves. I would be getting my first month's check of $50 soon and my brain was swirling with how I might spend it. The very next Saturday morning I returned alone to the shop. The Danglemeyer sisters greeted me warmly. "We're trying to get this display set up, so just look around as much as you'd like, won't you?" I was too young for some of the styles, I realized, but a black-and-white checked coat, small checks, caught my eyes. I lifted it off the rack. A wrap style polo coat, no buttons but with a long, wide belt. It was like a coat Kay Francis wore in a movie with George Brent. It was also expensive, $45.00! One of the Miss Danglemeyers came over to wait on me and I tried the coat on. It fit very well even if—at 5 feet, 1 ¾ inches—I looked nothing at all like tall, willowy Kay Francis in it. Miss Danglemeyer explained that I could put my purchase on layaway. Then she went over to the hat section and brought back a bright red-and-black patent leather hat! It was shaped like those straw sailor hats men wore in Summer. Did they call them "skimmers?" I loved the coat but wasn't as sure about the shape of the patent leather hat. Even if red is one of my favorite colors, the shape, that flat top made me look like a sawed-off tree stump. The managers of such a special shop as "La Parisienne", I thought, must know what they're doing. I'm quite sure, though, that Danglemeyer is <u>not</u> a French name. At any rate, I didn't like the hat, times-two.

When I got home, Mom was winding up the Saturday cleaning, so I fixed lunch. John was taking Mary to a Disney movie at the Majestic and Papa was giving him money for the afternoon: a nickel each for bus fare, fifteen cents for each movie ticket, a nickel apiece for Eskimo Pies. Vendors with trays of those treats strapped around their necks went through the theater at vaudeville time. Sometimes, instead, that nickel might have gone for a big, thick Holloway sucker, its rich caramel chewiness promising longer-lasting taste enjoyment.

Sometimes too, a vaudeville act like The Dixons followed the movie. A husband-wife team, Don Dixon played the country rube and Maisie, his glamour girl opposite. Not great theater, granted, but they did amuse our unsophisticated audience.

John and Mary caught the bus out in front of the house, Papa returned to the shop and Mama and I sat down to lunch. I had told her about my visit to La Parisienne with Jo and Gladys. I described for her the coat and hat I'd tried on that morning. She laughed at my description

16 By Fives to Ninety-five

of the patent leather hat and approved my decision not to buy it. "And, Mom, I can put the coat on lay-away and pay half of my first month's salary on it. I'd have it paid for in only two months!" Mom put her half-eaten tuna sandwich back on her plate, next to one of her home-canned dill pickle strips. She had that look parents get when they feel they have to straighten you out on some point. "My dear, when a family member starts earning money, the custom is to give a small portion of it "home" to help cover household expenses." She covered my hand with hers, seeming to sense my feeling of shame for not thinking of that myself. "I know you're eager to have lots of pretty new clothes, but you don't need them right away, do you?" I shook my head. "John has been wanting a motorcycle but he's been putting a share of his wages into "home", too. And, like him, you'll want to put a share of your earnings in a savings account." I did agree with Mom and together we worked out a plan. That night I dreamed I was riding behind John, my arms tight around his waist, on a shiny blue and silver motorcycle, up one of Dubuque's many steep hills. I was all dressed up in the black-and-white checked coat, cut to jacket length. The patent leather hat was secured with a striped dish towel under my chin. When we crossed the bridge over Catfish Creek, I pulled off the towel and sent the hat sailing—or skimming—into the creek.

   I'd been at National Refining close to three years when at a nearby lumber company, one of the secretaries told us that she would be leaving her job because she was pregnant and recommended me for the job. Five weeks later I found myself working as receptionist, switchboard operator and stenographer. Also, I would soon discover, as an unclassified checker-upper on a very able, usually personable bookkeeper, Jake. Jake seemed now and then to have small errors in balancing his books. He'd pass the huge, heavy ledgers along to me for checking and, with the near 20/20 vision of a nineteen-year old, I'd often come up with the problem. Jake started calling me "Sherlock Holmberg."

1938-1943

. . . an action-packed time span! It sped by as if set on "fast-forward." Loras had graduated from college in 1935 and had gone on to Sulpician Seminary at Catholic University in Washington, D.C. While he was in college, he'd been awarded silver medals twice in the annual French Oratorical Contest. I tried to write him every week or so during his four years in Washington. I thought he might get homesick. Also, it would be a good chance to try out my French. Miss Nelson, our French teacher, was pleased that we were doing this and helped me when I'd hit a snag. Loras wrote that he was "tres heureux" that I was getting high grades in French. I realized how hard he was studying, so I was also "tres heureux" that he wrote regularly, too.

In June 1939 Loras was ordained in our parish church, the Cathedral of St. Raphael. The newly ordained Father Loras would remain in Iowa to serve in the by-now archdiocese. Still a vast, sprawling area, more densely populated, of course, than in 1852 when our first bishop, Mathias Loras, had arrived to serve. The first bishop of the Dubuque diocese, Bishop Loras, had celebrated the first Mass offered in the yet-to-be-completed Cathedral on Christmas Day, 1857. Only twelve or so weeks later, in late February 1858 his death occurred. Born and educated in France, he had arrived in Dubuque about five years earlier. His diocese was a vast, sprawling section of the Great Northwest Territory, wild prairie country, inhabited by native Indians and small groups of immigrants. The new bishop had been so loved and respected by the people that many of them would give his family name, Loras, as the baptismal name to their newborn male infants.

18 By Fives to Ninety-five

In addition to my brother's priestly duties, he had another important priority: getting me into college, which he'd been encouraging for years. And a goal he quickly achieved.

The "non-traditional student" wasn't a common classification in those days. I was 21 but in only a few months I was enrolled as a freshman in Clarke's Food and Nutrition Department, with an emphasis on Hospital Dietetics. Since that major entailed, after completing college, a one-year internship in an accredited hospital, we worked out a three-year college plan. Heavy course loads during the three years at Clarke as well as at summer schools in between. A work-study program in the F & N Department. Plus clerking at J.C. Penney's on Main Street on most Saturdays, also on "Ember" or "Rogation" Days. Farmers marked the four change-of-season days during the year as holidays. Retailers advertised big sales to lure them into their stores, and needed additional help.

The work-study program in the F & N Department included, in fascinating part, assisting the department head, Sister Mary St. Clara Sullivan, with "The Kitchen of Tomorrow" broadcast from the F & N Department of Clarke over one of our two local radio stations. Sister planned, wrote the script for, produced and directed the weekly program. My assignment was to type and edit the script. An auditorium-type space adjoined the F & N Department. On the elevated stage a modern, functional demonstration kitchen was created, and comfortable space was provided for a live studio audience. An overhead demonstration mirror enabled attendees to see clearly what was going on, as Sister Mary St Clara, seated at a small side table, narrated helpful details. "Meanwhile, back at the range," one of Sister's upper classmen (This was in the days before gender sensitivity in language, remember?) was displaying her culinary skills. Depending on the complexities involved, the student might have an assistant.

Although not developed as a route to celebrity status for this dedicated educator or for the college, "The Kitchen of Tomorrow" had a long run, from 1938 through 1969. Tri-state area women became faithful supporters of the program, a truly _live_ studio audience! We students benefited in more ways than we realized at the time. In 1951, McCall's Magazine presented Sister an award "for public service in radio."

Because of my long-time interest in writing, I signed up for a class in Radio Script Writing, a first-time offering at Clarke. A wonderful instructor, Sister Mary Philippa Carr, a small class, and sheer fun. (Much more fun than my class in Geometry which followed, a math requirement I had to make up.) Another day student, a high school classmate of my brother John, and a sophomore, was on the work- study program, too. Phyllis Ullman was an honor student. Tall, energetic and generous with her time and know-how. She had hoped to go to medical school but faced financial barriers she couldn't surmount. I had had no science classes in high school and found Phyllis my lifeline when I was baffled by the mysteries of chemistry. Part of the problem, the instructor was a Displaced Person from Germany who spoke very little English. As hard as I'd study, her lecture the next morning was next-door to being completely lost on me. The situation, for her and for me, did ease somewhat after a few months. By the time I was taking a Bacteriology class in summer school, I began to feel like Madame Eve Curie.

As I was busy adapting to college, Father Loras was enjoying his role as assistant pastor at St. Matthew's in Cedar Rapids. Monsignor James Kearns was pastor and the soul of hospitality. An only child himself, he was delighted to have one—or often more—of our family or friends come to visit. Somewhat later, my brother was assigned as chaplain at a 52-bed Mercy Hospital in Anamosa. From there, he also served a mission in nearby Stone City, site of the Grant Wood's Art Colony during the early '40s. On visits to Father Loras in Anamosa, especially in the magnificent Midwest Fall and often on weekends, we attended Father's Sunday Mass in Stone City. Stone quarrying had been Anamosa's principal line of work and traces of that endeavor remained: deep valleys, hovering well-defined hills, incredible colors which Wood captured on canvas so faithfully. A typical New England colonial-style church stood out staunchly against the various hues of the blues and greens of the village's terrain. These visits were relaxing breaks from classes, study and exams. As were the occasional get togethers with former school-mates and my "working days" friends. The Clarke years were flashing by like greased lightning!

We all had circled Graduation Day in May of 1942 on every available calendar. But the awful Pearl Harbor attack by the Japanese on

December 7, 1941 lent a somber edge to our planning. Most of us had family and friends involved in the war in Europe, as were some recent Clarke graduates who were dietitians. My brother John had been drafted and entered the Army only six days before Pearl Harbor. Our brother Bill had entered earlier and was stationed at an Ordnance Depot in Herlong, California.

Of the current Food and Nutrition majors who would be graduating, some went into teaching, one into Consumer Service for a utility company and one into marriage. Eight of us had applied for dietetic internships. Each of us was limited to three applications and were eagerly awaiting another significant date, April 15, 1942. Responses from the hospitals where we had applied, with a separate, confidential appointment letter to the applicant enclosed, would have been sent to the Food & Nutrition Department heads at the involved colleges and universities. The appointment letters would be presented to the eight of us on the Big Day.

Early on April 15th we met for breakfast in the Department's Tea Room and for letter-opening, much jubilation and some disappointments! Promptly, as instructed by the American Dietetic Association, we notified the Association and the hospitals of our acceptances, or non-acceptances. This strategy provided "second chance" opportunities for students who may not have had an acceptance. For example, if you received two acceptances out of your three applications, your decision of which one to go with made the second acceptance a possible appointment for another student. Fortunately, I received appointments to the Johns Hopkins and the St. Louis University Hospitals. Both, excellent facilities, making my decision somewhat difficult, but it provided a happy opportunity for some other student. My appointment to the Johns Hopkins Hospital in Baltimore was to start on September 5, 1942. Only five months away!

With our internship acceptances tucked in our pockets, we felt airborne, eager for commencement in late May. But first there were term papers and other projects to complete, and studying for finals. For me, the turmoil of those weeks was greatly eased when my parents presented me with my class pin. A deep purple amethyst quarter-foil centered with the Clarke crest and encircled by little seed pearls.

I still had one more summer school session ahead. Luckily, right here at Clarke and with both classes in the morning. That allowed me four afternoons a week to work a part-time clerical job in a downtown Dubuque insurance agency. They were expanding and wanted assistance in the reorganization of materials and the setting up of a revamped filing system. Also, in handling business correspondence: taking—and faithfully transcribing—shorthand, then typing the letters for the manager's signing and getting them into the mail.

The owner-manager of the firm, Mr. Eberle, was interested in my job plans and we'd discussed them some. One of his daughters would be college age soon and wasn't sure what she wanted to do. How we veered into talking about personality traits, I don't know. I mentioned that I often have trouble making decisions, too. He chuckled. "I know that problem well. And I made myself learn to overcome it." He explained how he would take a little time to assess his choices, even in small things, and then make a firm, unchangeable decision. Although often tempted to change his mind, he stuck like a Band-aid to his decision. "I soon realized how much vacillating and mind-changing time I was spending." That chat was well-timed. As I prepared for my year in Baltimore, I had a lot of deciding to do. His strategy worked.

1943-1948

The excitement of the train trip from Dubuque to Chicago, the weekend there with my friends the Westcotts, and then on to Baltimore was only slightly diminished by the tearful farewells of my family and friends. We all understood that I wouldn't get home for a whole year. However, I was so revved up by advance helpful information mailed to me from Hopkins that I could hardly wait to get there. We arrived at 600 N. Broadway on September 7, of 1942—me and my very heavy tight–packed steamer trunk which, I now realized, was not intended for taxi cab transit. The dark red brick row house stood on the corner, directly across from the hospital entrance. Ginny Wright, a senior dietetic intern, welcomed me warmly when I rang the door bell. She guided the perplexed but persevering cabbie in extricating the problem monster and putting it in a basement storage room in the rear of "600."

The hospital, also dark red brick, is large and spreading, on a gently rising mini-mound of land a bit up from the wide sidewalk. A black wrought-iron fence beautifully outlines the Victorian style and dignity of the building. As you enter, a huge statue of Christ, arms outstretched, stands there in the middle of the reception area and welcomes you. On the base of the statue is the inscription, "Come unto me all ye who are weary and heavy-laden and I will give you rest." After meeting with Miss Phyllis Rove, Head of the Dietary Department, and her assistant, Miss Janet Engebretsen, the next few days were filled with job-starting details, registering with the hospital treasurer, arranging for uniform fitting, unpacking and settling in. I was chomping at the bit, eager for word of where my first assignment would be. That news came in a note from Miss Engebretsen late Wednesday afternoon, in clipped language not unlike Army orders: "Start Nurses Cafeteria 9 a.m. Thursday." Thursday? That was <u>tomorrow</u>!

Miss Buck, in charge of the Nurses' Cafeteria, welcomed me at 9 a.m. sharp and gave me a quick run-down of routines there. The meals, prepared in the Main Kitchen, and bussed down in large heated carts, were served under the supervision of Miss Buck and two dietetic interns to about 400 at breakfast and 600 at dinner and supper. Which required a split-shift work schedule—and very early a.m. starts—for the supervisors. The <u>standard</u> shift for dietetic interns was 6 to 11 a.m. and then back at 5 p.m. until 8 p.m. Hopkins custom dictated, we were informed, that you would always show up for duty at least 15 minutes early. Whether custom also dictated it, "quitting time" was almost always at least a half-hour later than scheduled. Part of the reason: the daily duties we had, in addition to meal service, for example, "count days." We would count dishes of all types one day a week; glassware the next day, and silver the next. Then we'd carefully record the counts in sturdy loose-leaf binders.

Another time-consuming duty was the "evening lock-up." With a ring of keys that would make a gatekeeper envious, the two interns, near the close of their 5 to 8 p.m. shift, would start on 3rd floor, in Main Kitchen. We'd check to insure that all perishable food and leftovers were properly stored, that range ovens and electric appliances were turned to the OFF mode and that refrigerator and freezer temperatures were in the specified range. Then down to the Bakery on 2nd floor for a check of refrigerators and storage rooms to be certain they were locked. And on to 1st floor, where Doctors' Dining Room was located, as were dining rooms for white and for colored employees. An important aspect of the check-up of Doctors' Dining Room was to be sure that one of the refrigerators in the adjoining kitchen was left unlocked and amply stocked for lunches or snacks by doctors around the clock.

With four weeks' experience in Nurses' Cafeteria chalked up, I started my next rotation in Main Kitchen on Monday. Miss Wetter, the head dietitian, gave me a brief familiarization tour of this "heart" of the hospital's food service. The meat and vegetable cookery area, the salad and the dessert sections, and even the "pot and pan room." Here Robert, a benign, smiling colored man interfaced all day long washing cumbersome, greasy cooking pans and never stopped smiling. A small section of the kitchen served as the Diet Kitchen, where physician-prescribed special diets were prepared for patients throughout the entire hospital.

The enormous amount of equipment in the Kitchen and the size of major pieces like soup kettles made me feel like a Lilliputian. When one worker, Hans, stopped stirring the contents of a gigantic soup kettle, Miss Wetter introduced us. A tall, middle-aged man, he and his family had escaped from Nazi Germany in the late thirties and he had found work at Hopkins, rapidly becoming a favorite of the whole Dietary Department.

Even though it meant getting up a 4:30 a.m. one day every week while assigned to Main Kitchen, I found the job of shopping for fruits and vegetables at wholesale market fascinating. One of the hospital drivers would pick up two of the interns at "600" at 5 a.m. and off we'd go to Chesapeake Bay. The marketers' colorful displays would be lined up in covered stalls along the waterfront—bushel basketfuls and crates of seasonal favorites like winter squash, turnips and eggplant, as well as all the stand-bys, cabbage, potatoes, etc. Vendors would proudly point out the high quality of the items as we evaluated them. They'd have ready answers for our questions. With melons, grapes, apples, etc., they'd offer samples which helped us in the overall evaluation—<u>and</u> also eased our hunger pangs. We usually checked with three or four vendors, jotting down prices from each one. Then back to "600," with enough time before meeting with Miss Wetter, to enjoy an un-sumptuous breakfast of graham crackers with peanut butter and mugs of the then fairly new but not yet perfected "instant coffee." Our meeting with Miss Wetter, going over the basic menus planned for the five weeks ahead. They were spread out on her desk-top, along with our comparative price figures charted on a large pad. With the benefit of Miss Wetter's practical experience, the meeting resembled a class in quantity food purchasing.

Main Kitchen was a demanding, challenging and rewarding rotation. After a few weeks, you were considered capable to substitute for the regular "senior" student on her day off. That assumed that she had had adequate time to thoroughly train her substitute. The "Senior student" was responsible for supervision of the loading, the checking and the issuing of the trucks.

From the day I'd left home for Baltimore in early September, I'd kept a detailed journal, as though I'd been sworn in under oath. By now our Fall internship group of eleven, whose arrivals had been intermittent, was complete: food and nutrition majors from colleges or universities in Ohio, Pennsylvania, Virginia, Iowa, Wisconsin and Illinois. Having been a day student at Clarke, this regional blend of housemates was a pleasant introduction to dorm-like living. Hopkins offered many excellent lectures which, as a teaching hospital, we were scheduled to attend. We also were fortunate to have classes on medical conditions where diet therapy was a significant or the principal treatment. Many of these were taught by former or present Hopkins medical staff, experts in their fields.

My third rotation would be coming up soon. And there were gaping blank spaces in the journal. A rainy day off gave me time for updating. A comment I'd written while still in Main Kitchen:

> "I'm beginning to feel that I know what it's all about! The thing is, by the time you feel you know all there is about the unit, you're moved to another unit. And once again, you're as green as grass. As Liza Doolittle would suggest, 'It does keep you 'umble!' "

Liza was right. Humble and with little time to dwell on details. In short, the rotation plan thus far went like this:

Nurses' Cafeteria

Main Kitchen

Osler 2—Colored Men's Ward

Thayer 2—Private Rooms

Actually getting onto a medical ward and in contact with real live (if ailing) patients made this assignment especially challenging. The Osler Wards were named for Doctor William Osler, one of the four founders of the hospital. Described as "a master observer of patients," Osler considered medicine as an art. He placed great value on the doctor-patient relationship. You could observe his philosophy on Osler 2. Many of the patients were advanced in age. Some of them appeared to have had little attention paid to their health or their nutritional needs. I was struck right away by how appreciative almost every patient was for the care he was receiving.

Osler 2 and Thayer 2 were separate duties under Rotation 3, and in separate buildings which necessitated rapid-dashing at least six times a day to accomplish service of the three daily meals. Dash #1, at 7:15 a.m. to Osler 2, where hopefully, breakfast had already been served by Nora Kelly, a relatively reliable colored woman. A check of Doctors' Order Book for any new orders or diet changes as well as a check of Kitchen supplies. Then, a resumption of the dashing, over to Thayer, where with the help of a staff aide, I'd serve breakfast at 8 a.m. (if the food cart from the Kitchen had gotten there on time). Some checking there before dashing over to the Ward office for reviewing menus for the following day, recording any changes I had noted and, if time allowed, getting a start on writing diets for a few days ahead. Otherwise, I'd do them when off duty. Around 11 a.m. it was a dash down to Osler for the main meal and then over to Thayer 2 to serve dinner at 12.

Patient visiting, which provides valuable feedback when a patient rates the food, was sandwiched in before going off duty "around" 1 p.m., more than ready to eat a bite and take a nap. As I dozed off a rash of thoughts raced through my mind. Use of a colored patient's first name only, or of his last name without the prefix "Mr." was difficult for me to adjust to. As was their polite, soft dialect. Did they have any problem understanding me, I wondered? Recent comments about my "Midwestern" accent had surprised me. Back to the hospital at 5 p.m. (indeed, at 4:45, in compliance with the Hopkins custom). Supper on Osler 2—or was it, perhaps Nora, the maid—was running late? Every now and then she would have nipped some spirits on her afternoon break and her balance, let's say, was unpredictable. After my dash over to Thayer 2, their 6 p.m. supper went smoothly, even leaving a little time for chats with two or three patients.

Osler 4—White Men's Ward

What a relief, when assigned to Osler 4, to learn that it would be a single ward rotation! The Osler 2—Thayer 2 rotation had kept me hopping. It had been interesting and challenging but left little time for worthwhile patient contact. Although there were some run-of-the-mill cases on Osler 4, the majority were serious, often life-threatening. A case I've never forgotten, was Peter Medzinski, 69, an organ-grinder, whose music brightened the atmosphere along elite Charles Street, come rain or shine.

One day shortly before noon, he suddenly blacked out and slumped to the sidewalk. His assistant, a lively little monkey called "Sammy," and a crowd of their Charles Street fans, stood watch as ambulance aides picked Peter up and rushed him to the Emergency Room at Hopkins. Peter's skin was as hardened and smooth as the shells on Chesapeake Bay clams. Routine preliminary lab tests confirmed what seemed obvious. Peter was weak, anemic and severely malnourished. He was transferred to Olser 4.

When word of the diagnosis of scurvy spread throughout the hospital, Peter's room became as if magnetized. Doctors, Residents, Interns, Dietitians, Nurses stopped by to observe what this "ancient" malady looked like. It had been a scourge in sea-faring days, when sailors were ship-bound for months and deprived of fruits and vegetables rich in vitamin C as well as other essential nutrients.

The next morning I was eager to visit with the patient and query him on what a typical day's food intake might be. He was a gentleman and a gentle man, sharing the information without hesitation, even with a trace of pride in his independence. Even on Osler 4, where "Mr. Medzinski" would be the rule, he insisted on being called "Peter." Since he observed Sunday as a day of rest, he'd spend a little time preparing his "meals" for the entire week ahead. On Saturday he would buy—and hard-boil—a dozen eggs to have ready in the icebox for 2-a-day consumption, with a wiener and a couple slices of white bread, every day but Sunday. "A can of sardines in mustard sauce is my Sunday treat." He smiled and added, "I always buy a banana for Sammy's Sunday treat. For Peter himself there were never any fruits or fruit juices, never any vegetables. He described a large enamel-ware coffee pot (which had been his mother's) speckled dark blue and white. He'd make a full pot of coffee, to be reheated daily during the entire week ahead. And that had been the meal pattern for close to 25 years!

A treatment plan was immediately set in motion by the physicians in charge, with valuable input from dermatology, dietary and dental departments. So much collateral damage like spongy gums and missing or defective teeth made drinking orange, tomato, grapefruit or other juices far from enjoyable. Eating high-vitamin C vegetables in the cabbage family (except for sauerkraut!) was also difficult. The recovery path for Peter Medzinski would be long and bumpy. But he was an example of patience and perseverance. He'd keep a return with Sammy to Charles Street as his goal!

Marburg Private Pavilion

My fifth rotation—to Marburg, a separate wing off the hospital's main corridor, with large rooms overlooking green lawns and a few lingering Fall flowers and berry bushes. It was mid-December. I'm sure that at home the ground would be snow-covered. My "600" next door neighbor, "Cott," had already served her Marburg stint. She told me that Miss Helene Barbee, head of the Marburg Dietary, was not a dietitian, but a recognized authority on food and "matters culinaire." She had traveled widely here and abroad, apparently with the means to master the art of fine dining. She was buxom, aristocratic looking, with beautiful auburn hair. Instead of the classic white uniform which dietitians wore, Miss Barbee favored a long white lab coat.

The major components of the 80 to 100 meals served three times a day from the Marburg 4th floor kitchen had been prepared right there. Under the supervision of a graduate dietitian and the dietetic intern, servers plated the foods to conform to the patients' pre-checked diet slips, put the trays on a dumbwaiter and sent them to the floors below. Nurses' aides then promptly served them to patients. In the effort to keep the food at the desirable temperature and to maintain its taste quality, rapid action and careful attention to the entire process was essential. On a Sunday evening, when the graduate dietitian was off and I was substituting for her, time was suddenly catching up on me. As though it was the 11th Commandment, I'd observed the cardinal rule of tasting every main menu component before plating was started and had decided that a couple of items didn't require it. In general, however, all went smoothly, thanks be.

"All went smoothly," I had thought. On Monday, when I was working 8 to 1 and 4 to 7, I learned otherwise. Miss Barbee came on in mid-morning and was there only briefly when she summoned me. "Miss Holmberg, we've received an oyster stew complaint. Did you taste the oyster stew before you began tray service?" It had been one of the items I'd considered "skippable." "No, Miss Barbee, I didn't." She shook her head in disapproval before directing me to go back to the kitchen and get any oysters that might be there and bring them up to her desk. I took a lone chipboard container from the shelf. I opened it to find three sour-smelling oysters slithering around in the bottom. I closed the container tight and hurried to her desk with it. There she had a small plate, a fork and napkin set up for my sampling of the evidence. As soon as she removed the container's lid, an awful whiff of its contents gave her second thoughts. She called for Jackson, one of the cook's helpers, to dispose of the closed container immediately. Fearing that she might extend that order to include me, I started to explain the time pressures, not intending it to be an alibi. Miss Barbee was more adept. She sensed my uneasiness. "Rules are for a reason. They're made to be kept. We're fortunate that the nurse's aide on second was alert. She detected an off-odor when she started serving the few trays that included the stew and provided several other choices to the patients." I thanked Miss Barbee for her understanding and counsel.

Baltimore's proximity to Washington, especially during wartime, brought many high-ranking army and navy figures to Marburg. Their privacy was carefully guarded, but I do recall the hospital-wide excitement upon hearing that Brigadier General Patrick Jay Hurley had been admitted. As personal representative of President Franklin D. Roosevelt, he served as minister to New Zealand and visited the Near East, the Middle East, China and Iran. In 1944 he was appointed U.S. Ambassador to China.

New York wasn't far away from our hospital either and many famous persons—writers, stars of stage and screen, outstanding athletes—would appear as patients <u>and</u> on the front pages in those pre-television days, when "celebs" were becoming a dime a dozen. Only occasionally, would a dietetic intern have any contact with these patients. Many of them had engaged private-duty R.N.s to care for them around the clock. But fortune smiled broadly at us when Josephine Sherwood Hull, the stage star for whom the play "Arsenic and Old Lace" was written, was admitted to Johns Hopkins. The play had an extended Broadway run and, when filmed ran in movie and community theaters over the entire country. A 5' 2¼' woman in her mid-sixties, she was most noted and loved for her comedy and drama roles. Described in one publicity release as "short and dumpy of build," that unflattering image was counter-balanced by her verve and warmth. She was one of the most interesting and personable individuals I've ever met. She'd played in other Broadway hits such as "You Can't Take It With You" and "Harvey," for which she won an Academy Award for her role as supporting actress. Very soon she had become exhausted and came to Hopkins for a check-up. Our dietary department was involved, of course, in her treatment plan. Either the senior intern or I would visit Mrs. Hull daily and tailor menus to her taste and her nap schedule. Her energy level rose quickly. When diagnosed with mild diabetes, her lifestyle did present tactical problems. At that time, insulin was administered sub-cutaneously, right before the meal. But like many performers, she preferred not to eat a heavy or even a light meal right before a performance. "I like to nibble a few nut meats before I go on, and sometimes between acts," she explained. Since she would be requiring insulin only once a day, we assured her that we could work out a few meal patterns that would accommodate that practice.

Mrs. Hull was a joy to visit with, a people-person, eager to know more about others. She asked about my family. When I mentioned that Father Loras had always longed to become an actor, that in high school and in college, he was in almost every play produced there. On one of his bedroom walls he had displayed a typical large poster used in those days to promote attendance. Almost as prominent as the play's title, "The Dead of Night," by Eugene O'Neill, was the elegantly written signature, "starring Gordon Grandfield," his chosen stage name. "Grandfield" is a family name from Mother's ancient past. "Gordon," a school and college friend. Josephine was amused. "I'm glad he chose the priesthood, dear. I've always respected and admired your church so much. Its beauty and dignity. Its steadfast adherence to moral principles and its concern for the poor. I often visit St. Patrick's, your cathedral, here in New York for rejuvenation!"

The Marburg rotation extended throughout Christmas time and was high-lighted by a Hopkins Christmas Eve tradition that <u>almost</u> made up for my missing Christmas at home. Hopkins staff members, including residents and interns, met at 6:30 p.m. in the reception area around the base of the statue of Christ. We proceeded throughout the entire hospital singing Christmas carols. On many of the public wards, both white and colored, smiling patients with tear-filled eyes joined in. Carols never sounded more beautiful.

After the Marburg assignment, rotations seemed to take place—and to be completed—more rapidly.

Halsted 2—Colored Men's Surgical Ward

Like Osler 2, Halsted 2 had a few commonplace cases but predominating were complex ones affecting men of various ages. These presented welcome challenges to the surgical staff. One of these was Willie Taylor who, as a curious 3-year-old toddler, had drunk from a bottle of lye and suffered a severely burned esophagus. He'd been an "in-and-out" Hopkins patient for the following 15 years, while an artificial esophagus, correlated with predicted and actual changes in his growth pattern, was being constructed. Fifteen years of meticulously planned tube feedings to meet his nutritional needs, and for Willie, many periods of pain and discomfort.

Willie was eighteen when I encountered him and interested in all aspects of his treatment. Occasionally, with the approval of his doctors we would treat him to a 'burger or a ham sandwich—with an emesis basin to catch its contents after the chewing and expectorating.

Halsted 5—White Women's Ward

Tray service on this rotation demanded less of the intern's attention because "Ventress" was (firmly) "in charge." She had started part-time in Nurses' Cafeteria as a teen-ager, dropping out of school not long after. By the time we'd met, she'd been a Halsted kitchen maid for a good number of years. Efficient and conscientious, she was also the loving mother of two teen-age daughters and grandmother of their three children. When, a few months after that New Year's Day, twin boys arrived to the younger daughter, name-choosing presented little indecision. Grandma Ventress was a regular patient at the hospital's dental clinic and, with boundless enthusiasm exclaimed, "Let's call them "Oral Hygiene" and "Oral Eugene!"

Ventress was an asset in creating for us more time for patient interaction, and for diet instruction when called for. I recall so vividly, visits with four-year-old "Janie," born with her bladder outside her body. With two surgeries behind her and the possibility of a third looming, her interest in meals was minimal. I would make it a point to stop to see her at tray-time—and to wear a pair of small dome shaped bright blue cuff links which fascinated her—as I cajoled her into trying spoonfuls of this or that.

Although not a part of our rotation, a Burn Ward was located in the Halsted Building, also. Patients were admitted from the Chemical Warfare Arsenal in nearby Edgewood, Maryland. So severely burned were most of them that they were suspended, hammock style, over their beds with the goal of easing their pain and discomfort. Another major challenge was to overcome the stench of burnt human flesh.

Hopkins Food Clinic

Two outward differences between Food Clinic and our other rotations were pleasant. First, not needing to get up in the middle of the night to make it when on early duty in Nurses' Cafeteria. And second, instead of our standard white uniforms, we wore street clothes and white lab coats. Unlike in the Midwest, Spring in Baltimore can be counted on to arrive early and to merge as by magic into Summer.

The Clinic was structured of small private offices fitted for friendly, informal meetings with patients. Patients who were most often accompanied by a family member or friend who might understand and remember the dietitian's message. Often, mothers or grandmothers would have small charges in tow.

Mrs. Eloise Trescher, the wife of a Hopkins staff surgeon, headed the Clinic and was an effective and gentle teacher. Her basic mantra was to try to understand the patient, "to get inside his or her skin." To use simple, understandable language and not an excess of words. Avoid being condescending or patronizing.

We counseled numerous weight loss and diabetic patients, as well as many on sodium restricted plans. Always the great need was to emphasize the importance and benefits of well-balanced, nutritious meals and of healthy snacks. "Rosie," one of our 50-ish diabetic ladies, was a fervent gum chewer. At a time when sugarless gum was relatively rare. I reminded her that one stick—and certainly a package—of gum gave her a sugar-load she didn't need, she responded with a broad grin. "Oh, honey, don't you worry. My husband chews all the sugar out of it before he gives it to me!"

The internship year was winding down and life was busy. A few more class sessions, attendance at a meeting of the State Dietetic Association at the University of Maryland, and a dinner at Hopkins honoring our graduating interns and those of other local hospitals. In the midst of all this excitement we were all weighing the "what's next?" matter. My two "600" next-door neighbors and I had been invited to remain on the staff there: Arlene in a metabolic research lab, Cott in Marburg and I as an instructor in the hospital's School of Nursing. We mulled the decision over, inviting other interns for cocoa and cookies and for their views.

Things seemed to fall into place when one of our good friends would be completing his residency and going on to a fellowship on the West Coast. With his wife and infant son, he was vacating an apartment a mere three blocks from the hospital. Best known as one of several "Hopkins apartments" because it had been an ideal "stopover" for so many hospital staff members seeking convenient, temporary housing. It was _not_ spacious—one bedroom, a living room, with kitchen and a bath, each about the size of a small clothes closet, right off it.

A more accurate name for the apartment would be a "flat," up over Deckelbaum's Butcher Shop. The owner had died and the shop was run by his widow and their older son Howard. Access was by way of an enclosed stairway sandwiched in between the butcher shop, and their adjoining living quarters and the garage. In those days, butcher shops were still "in vogue." Carcass meat would be delivered to the shop where the butcher would do all the cutting: on a customer's order or to display briefly in his only refrigerated meat case. Either way there were bones a-plenty to stash in tall metal garbage cans in the garage, with garbage pickup time a week later. The result: a "perfumed" entry which was definitely _not_ Chanel No. 5!

We adapted to our new abode quickly. We had more important things to think about. Family members and many friends in the service and too often, long stretches when there was not a word from them. And what a bright day when word did come! Howard Deckelbaum was exempt from service because of his mother's dependence on him. His brother had enlisted early in the Marines. Howard was delighted too, that the mail had come through. He placed each piece or two in the corner of one of the steps leading up to our apartment. The discovery when we came off would make us want to sing out the opening song from "Oklahoma"—"Oh, what a beautiful morning!"

The year of internship at the Johns Hopkins Hospital, followed by teaching at their School of Nursing, was punctuated by strong pulls to enlist in the U.S. Army Women's Medical Specialist Corps, pulls which I could no longer resist. I faced strong opposition from my father. "Your two brothers were drafted and had to go. You don't." Although Mother didn't cheer my action, I do believe she understood how I felt.

This branch of the Army included physical therapists and occupational therapists as well. We were commissioned second lieutenants and quartered in comfortable, if somewhat monastic barracks adjoining the hospitals we would be serving.

My introduction to military life was six early-Spring weeks of rigorous basic training in COLD, colorful Colorado Springs. Drill grounds were in the shadow of snow-capped Pike's Peak, an awesome sight as dawn is breaking. On completion of those six weeks, we were transferred to Medical Replacement Pools—MRPs—to await orders. My MRP was at O'Reilly General Hospital in Springfield, Missouri. The orders came only four or five days later. As I read the spare-the-words message, "To Moore General Hospital, Swannanoa, North Carolina by June 2, 1945," I envisioned hot, sticky weather, buzzing mosquitoes, swamps and hungry crocodiles. A doctor-friend at O'Reilly who'd served at Moore, enlightened me. "It's in the foothills of the Smokies, 10 miles or so west of Asheville. It's called 'the country club of the South,' a plum of an assignment!"

Moore General was a treatment center for patients, most of them male, being returned from the South Pacific Theater. Men suffering from a variety of horrible tropical diseases, of which our medics had

36 By Fives to Ninety-five

limited experience. Some of the patients were emaciated, their livers almost completely destroyed. Some had been Japanese prisoners of war. Diet therapy was an integral part of their treatment. One GI, 28, a staff sergeant, was no longer emaciated. As a prisoner of war for a number of years, he had been so deprived of food that his weight had fallen from 165 to 58 pounds. When released, he wolfed down any food he met and when he had come to Moore, his weight was approaching 200 pounds. Restricting his food choices was an ironic challenge. But he was an amiable, compliant patient, and we were successful.

One other patient was an entirely different challenge. A lieutenant colonel on the psychiatric ward, in his forties and ambulatory. Having never tasted Philadelphia Scrapple, a blend of cooked cornmeal, ground sausage and seasonings, molded into loaves or "bricks" and refrigerated or frozen. To prepare, it's sliced, dredged lightly in flour and sautéed in drippings or cooking oil. The scrapple impressed the officer so much when he ate it the first time, that he came to believe that he himself had invented it. He wrote me a note asking if he could come by the Mess Hall Office and discuss initiating proceedings for applying for a patent on his scrapple. I consulted with one of the staff psychiatrists before responding. What would he think about inviting the officer to a simple scrapple and scrambled egg breakfast in the Mess Hall? If that psychiatrist could come, and maybe another dietitian, we might be able to convince the L.C. that scrapple has enjoyed a long run. As worthy, if not as inevitable as grits, a breakfast favorite in the South. Although it took two breakfast reruns, the strategy did prove effective.

The wars in both European and South Pacific theaters were winding down and realignment of forces became the name of the game. Much to my dismay I was ordered to leave my beloved Smokies for Fort Bragg in Eastern North Carolina. I found my brief stint there among paratroopers and not too far from the awesome Atlantic Ocean fascinating. Where dietary treatment was concerned, I realized that broken bones were usually less challenging than tropical diseases! From Fort Bragg I was transferred to Fort McClellan, Alabama for even a shorter stint. Victory in Europe (V-E Day), May 8, 1945 had been celebrated with great jubilation and relief. Celebration of V-J Day, August 14, 1946, was with great relief but with the indelible memory for all Americans of the outrageous assault on Pearl Harbor. At Fort McClellan, and as a commissioned officer, I was "separated" from the U.S. Army without much adieu. (That term, "separated" was more familiar to me when used in a culinary context.) Not having earned any impressive medals, ribbons or stars, and lacking any combat experience to relate, my transition to civilian life was without pageantry. I had missed my Midwest lifestyle, so I returned to Dubuque, deciding to checkout hospital dietetic positions in Chicago and Minneapolis, where I had good friends. Family and friends extended "a heroine's welcome," of course. My father particularly was relieved of his fears for my safety. And for my being thrust into undesirable situations. I assured him that many of my Army friends have remained my greatest and most enduring veteran's benefit.

Coming shadow-close to accepting a job in Chicago, I was side tracked by a phone call from Julia Jean ("J.J.") Wallace, also a Dubuquer and a Clarke classmate. She'd been a therapeutic dietitian at the 300 bed St. Thomas Hospital in Nashville for a few years and we'd kept in touch. The head dietitian there had resigned to help care for a seriously ill husband. J.J. promptly talked to the hospital administrator, Sister Lydia Hoffman, and told her about me, my availability and my possible interest in the St. Thomas job. Sister Lydia called me the next day for a very long, pleasant Ma Bell phone interview. The "possible" interest increased. I sent Sister my résumé and brief biographical information. Within a few days a letter came from her including folders on the hospital and on the Nashville area. Two weeks later I was boarding a train into Chicago, then transferring to one going on to "the Athens of the South."

Thanks to J.J.'s thoughtfulness, temporary housing awaited my Nashville arrival on a hot, humid Thursday evening in late August. A furnished upstairs apartment in a welcoming old brick home only two blocks from St. Thomas and across the street from Vanderbilt College campus. Mr. and Mrs. Drake, the retired owners, occupied the spacious first floor. J.J. and her friend Dan met me at the train station. We stopped for supper and a happy catch-up visit on our way to the apartment.

On Friday, a 9 A.M. meeting with Sister Lydia in her office started the day. It also marked the beginning of a privileged association with this remarkable woman. Her religious order, The Daughters of Charity of St. Vincent de Paul, had been founded in France in 1663, almost three centuries ago. Today, their mission remains the same: to care for the poor and needy. When founded, their habit was "the simple garb of the French peasant woman." Over the centuries modifications had been made. But as Sister Lydia rose from her desk to greet me that morning, I saw a woman of competence as well as compassion. She was wearing a simple floor-length dress of deep blue. Her head-piece was the same as was worn by the mid-1600s French peasant woman, and a lightly starched white linen "coronet." Because of the flexibility of the head-pieces and their resemblance to birds in flight, the Daughters of Charity are often lovingly referred to as "God's geese."

Our visit was informative and Sister's welcome to me, warm and friendly. Then it was tour time. First, of course, the Dietary Department and then, through the entire hospital. Tour conductor was Sister Lydia, not an assignee. She introduced every employee by name, and gently drew them into brief chats about their jobs. Then, without fail, she'd add a few words of appreciation for their work and its value to the hospital.

We started in the kitchen, to get ahead of the busy dinner service, loading of the food carts to be bussed up to the four floors of patients. Happily, we were in time to inhale the tempting aromas of the food being prepared. Aromas which also lured discerning hungry flies in this limited air conditioning era.

After lunch we toured the rest of the hospital. But not before taking time for me to meet Gabriella, the recently-hired assistant in the Dietary office. A 17-year-young immigrant married to Charles Johnson, a Canadian G.I. They had met during the War in Rome, her home-town. Now a veteran, he was attending Vanderbilt in preparation for law school. Gabriella's language skills were minimal. In fact, sub-minimal. Her eagerness and determination to master English were challenged by her difficulty in understanding the deep Southern accents which surrounded her daily. But she was bright, enthusiastic and efficient. Also, although not a requirement for her job, she was beautiful. Sparkling dark eyes, chestnut-brown hair braided coronet-style. She looked like an artist's model for a very young Madonna. Whenever introductions were in order, the Dietary staff loved asking Gabriella to give her full name. With grace, she was quick to comply.

"Gabriella Maria Isabella Jeannetta Rizzuto Johnson." Like a bubbling brook, the names rolled merrily off her tongue.

Having had such a pleasant, interesting Friday orientation to my new job, the entire weekend stretched out before me. J.J. and two of her friends had shifted into Southern hospitality mode and quickly filled the calendar. First, they ordered me to sleep late on Saturday, an idea I endorsed without quibbling. Then, if I'd like, shopping. Dinner at "Hundred Oaks," a charming restaurant set in a restored colonial mansion on the fringes of Nashville. After late Mass on Sunday, a scrumptious brunch for the four of us at J.J.'s apartment. Followed by touring the city and beautiful surrounding area. These thoughtful, gracious women could not have done more to make my move easier!

On Monday I was ready and eager to navigate the currents and depths of the hospital's Dietary Department. How pleased I was to see first-hand what a well organized and equipped, smooth-running department my predecessor appeared to have managed! And now, in 1947, in the still segregated South, her predominately "colored," as well as white employees came across as well-trained, comfortable and happy in their jobs. In my time at Hopkins, I had interfaced with many blacks, of course. And in North Carolina and Alabama, where I'd served as hospital dietitian in the Army hospitals, segregation was certainly in full effect. Having grown up in Dubuque, then a town of about 40,000 where only two highly respected black families lived, these horizons were totally different—and challenging. For example, "the Annie case." One "Annie," a top-notch black assistant cook, about 45, who had not finished grade school, worked in the main kitchen. Another Annie, a white woman of the same age and perhaps slightly higher educational level, was in charge of the Nurses' Cafeteria, and was automatically called "<u>Miss</u> Annie." As I started the routine check of the cafeteria food line one day a little before dinner, large pans of hot food had just been set in the steam table and weren't yet covered. And there was Miss Annie with her spray gun, armed to shoot the contents over the food. I caught her—and the gun—in time. Before I could launch into a strong reprimand, she smiled and patted my arm. "Don't you worry, honey, there's no spray in the gun." She looked like the man in a 1940's ad for the sure-fire fly spray, "FLIT." The ad caption: "Quick, Henry, the "Flit"!"

After a few months at St. Thomas Hospital, I was convinced that on balance, department harmony was at a noticeably high level. <u>Mr</u>. Webb, the chef, and his top assistant, "Robert", I'd soon learned, had a surprising and broad knowledge of food and its preparation. They recognized the responsibility of feeding their "family" of 300 patients and worked together as a team. They were cooperative, ready to take directions and offer suggestions. A specific "suggestion incident" is etched in my memory.

We planned menus on a 6-week cycle. Then I'd review them with <u>Mr</u>. Webb and "Robert." On a winter cycle including Christmas and New Year's Day, Christmas featured "Roast Turkey and the Trimmin's"—unanimous approval. For January First: "Baked Ham, Sweet Potatoes, etc." Right away I sensed a negative in the air. "Miss Holmberg, everybody would be terribly disappointed if we didn't have Ham Hocks and Black-eyed Peas! Eating them on New Year's Day brings you good luck for the whole year!" <u>Mr</u>. Webb's words of warning were seconded by "Robert." Averse to causing such cruel disappointment and prolonged ill fortune, I conceded. They looked relieved and agreed with my suggestion to offer an alternate choice. "Roast Beef, perhaps?"

Mr. Cockrell, with years of bakery experience, appreciated "Mary," his very capable helper. So did the Salad and Dessert Room ladies, <u>Mrs</u>. DeMoss, <u>Mrs</u>. Ryder and <u>Miss</u> Evans, a young woman working hard to support her widowed mother and teen-age brother. The women worked closely with the Bakery and were, all of them, fond of Mary. They hated her having to fight her way to the back of the bus every day and suffering other such indignities.

"Loyal", in charge of the storeroom, was justifiably proud of how shiny-clean and orderly the large storage space was. When Sister Lydia commented, "And Loyal always lives up to his name . . ." he beamed like a battery-fed glowworm. (And, I thought, I could glow right along with him, to inherit such a staff!)

1948–1953

In late summer of 1949, Sister Mary St. Clara, head of the Food and Nutrition Department at Clarke, was faced with a critical medical problem requiring immediate surgery. A year's leave from teaching was ordered by her physician. In those days and particularly with consecrated religious, such matters were considered what they are: highly personal. The college contacted me, inquiring whether I could possibly substitute for Sister for the school year. We met without delay to discuss the situation—quietly and quickly. I'm convinced that life presents us with situations where a negative response is simply not possible. So in September of 1949, I launched my best efforts as a substitute for our dear Sister St. Clara. Clarke was still a small private women's college, with registration ranging from 350 to 400. The Food and Nutrition Department that year included students who'd set their sights on teaching, hospital dietetics, or, a few, on a job in the consumer service department of a business or utility. There were half a dozen seniors who would be applying for hospital internships.

That process started early in the school year and was an anxious, exciting time for the young applicants—<u>and </u>for their substitute instructor. April 15, 1950 would end the suspense. In the meantime, I was becoming aware of how much I was learning from the underclassmen. At age 31 I was interacting daily with students witnessing the beginning of an era of significant strides in developing new food products. I sensed that some of these students had never gone beyond baking a pizza or heating a can of soup. I recall the puzzlement on the face of one bright, above-average sophomore during a discussion of watchguards to observe when blending an acid ingredient into an alkaline mixture. As an example, I used the preparation of Cream of

Tomato Soup. Clearly, Meg had never known, or even heard of anyone who's prepared that stand-by "from scratch." There were other students, especially some with rural backgrounds who had participated in 4-H or other such programs and were food and nutrition savvy and enthusiastic. The school year whipped by. April 15th brought five of our six internship applicants the acceptances they'd hoped and prayed for. The sixth applicant was awarded two alternates, one of which became an acceptance the next day.

Sister St. Clara's surgery had been successful and her recuperation went smoothly. She'd be back at the podium in the Fall of 1950. I was eager to tend to the "writing bug" which wasn't entirely satisfied with lesson plans, grading exams and evaluating term papers.

Dubuque's proximity to Chicago and my familiarity with the City's four newspapers, prompted me to write first to the food editor of Chicago's Herald American. I'd heard her speak at a State Dietetics Association meeting a few years before. She was an Iowan, an Iowa State graduate. (She bore the very same name as Dorothy C. Thompson, the famous journalist.) She set up an interview in Chicago for the next week and, by late Summer, I had become a news reporter. Mrs. Thompson headed a staff of seven and wasted no time initiating me into the basics of newspaper food writing. She was generous with assignments, coached me on journalistic ins and outs and included me in press parties which usually yielded a story. Her right-hand, indispensable assistant was Cora Beman. She was of middle-European descent and a human treasury of food knowledge. She and I had abutting king-size desks, and our phones rang endlessly with culinary or household-related questions. The Chicago area's multi-ethnic population brought us numerous hard-to-understand calls, which at the start I turned over to my "Cora colleague." Her responses were always gracious, her explanations simple and understandable. Cora lived in suburban Maywood as did her son, Bob, a Civil War buff, and his wife, Linda, and baby. Often on weekends, I'd enjoy Maywood hospitality and great conversation about the Civil War battle sites and books in general. Cora was my valued mentor and a cherished friend throughout the rest of her life.

One unforgettable assignment in my "newspaper career" was a six-week feature, TRUDY'S DIET, described as "a slimming program" for the fictional Trudy. It was based on a 1200-calorie daily diet, nutritionally sound, no frills. It hinged on the combined efforts of the food, beauty and fashion editors, with regular input from "the dietitian." Daily progress notes from Trudy were front-page news in our paper. In the fourth week of the feature, returning late from a Saturday night date, we picked up a Sunday "American." The headline blared: TRUDY LOSES 4 MORE POUNDS! The 6-week feature did achieve the hoped-for goal of a newspaper sales spurt. I trust that Trudy fans found in the feature a lasting route to sound, effective weight control.

I managed to do a little writing on the side and sold a short story and a magazine non-fiction piece. At that time a report on the declining health of William Randolph Hearst, publisher of the Chicago paper and owner of the Hearst Castle near San Simeon, California, appeared frequently. (Along with repeated conjecturing about whether England's Princess Margaret would marry Group Captain Peter Townsend.) So the announcement of staff cutbacks at Hearst's Chicago paper came as no surprise.

Mrs. Thompson had asked me to accompany her one afternoon on a shopping trip to a top-notch Stop 'n Shop supermarket nearby to gather information for a regular weekly column which she and I wrote. On our rainy return cab ride back and protected with plastic rain bonnets, we must have resembled members of the foreign legion. She took my hand and poured out the bad news. She was going to have to cut her staff by three. Unfortunately, I would have to be one of the three. "But I've already talked with friends, the heads of Armour's Consumer Service, Swift's Home Economics Department, and the Poultry and Egg National Board. They each want you to come for an interview. They'll be expecting your phone call." I was touched by her concern and by the considerate cut-back's delay of a month. That gave me time for the three interviews, and more if needed—and decision making. (Women heading consumer service departments for major food and equipment manufacturers, usually have a trade name, such as Betty Crocker, Martha Logan, Ann Pillsbury.) All three interviews fell within the following week. The first one, with Esther Latzke, Armour's "Marie Gifford," was almost too good to be true. The very week before, a staff vacancy had occurred, a position with emphasis on editorial work. It included development of educational materials, editing of all recipes and press releases generated in the department, and the planning and setting up of food photos. Miss Latzke had headed the department for years. She felt that my background would meet the requirements of the vacant position and offered me the job. I started work at Armour in December of 1951.

Most of the major meat packers had their general offices and slaughter operations in "the Yards." Admittedly, the slaughter operation lent an odoriferous note to the area. But once inside our Consumer Service Department, you could inhale deeply! And Jennie, a mature housekeeper in the Test Kitchen, wasn't hesitant about commenting, in her soft Scottish burr, "Remembuh, it's youhr bread and buttah!"

1953-1958

Our family was "genetically celebratory." There was always something to celebrate. Foremost was the inherent appreciation of God's greatest gift—the gift of life itself. An abundance of birthdays. In this time span, the weddings of my sisters, Mary in early September of 1953 and Helen, in April of 1956. And then in June of 1958, the Golden wedding celebration for our parents, with the entire family sharing their gratitude and joy. Gratitude and joy which we all experienced when Mary and Noel's first child, Christopher James Walsh, arrived in late September of 1954. And almost three years later, his little sister, Mary Elizabeth. (Her charmed father very soon started calling her "Mary Boo.")

All these celebrations had helped me ease into my new job with Armour. Previously I'd been used to walking to work. Now closeness to the work site from home was <u>not</u> one of the many pluses of the job. I was living on Chicago's near-north side, in the "old St. Michael" section settled by German immigrants. Off and on car-pooling worked pretty well. Or otherwise, I'd board the "L" at Fullerton for the trip to the Yards. In next to no time, the "L" would descend into the subway, quickly snake through Chicago's Loop, then emerge and continue south to the Indiana and Hyde Park stops. There, stockyard employees transferred to a train which served the various stockyard companies. It was sort of a "Toonerville Trolley."

Armour's general office was across the street from a large building housing the slaughtering and packing operations. The Consumer Service Department and a Bakery Research Laboratory occupied the first floor there. Our department included an office section for the Chicago staff of eight graduate home economists and two clerical assistants. In addition, four regional "Marie Giffords," lived and served in the Midwest, Northeast, Southeast and West Coast. To the left of our staff's narrow rectangular office section, there was a wonderfully utilitarian area, which led to the Bakery Research Lab. The space facilitated a variety of meetings, taste panels, product presentations, and a considerable amount of black and white food photography. Also, I learned this first week of my early December start, the staging of a delightful Christmas tea. General Office department heads, researchers, photographers, and other colleagues with whom we worked closely were the annual guests.

The Consumer Test Kitchen, geared to the home preparation of food, was right next to the Staff Office. An office for director of the department, Miss Latzke, and her secretary was on the other side of the kitchen.

Our department assisted on a project with Bakery Research which made coming to work a gustatory pleasure. A Chicago bakery and Armour customer, Sara Lee, was developing a coffee cake for the frozen food market, an old-fashioned type in a round foil pan. Made from yeast dough and rich with chopped pecans and light butter-cream frosting, it resembled a one-layer dessert cake and tasted like manna from Heaven.

When the bakery formula for the product won unanimous approval by Sara Lee, we tested numerous samples to arrive at the oven temperature and length of baking time which insured best eating quality. Along with these preparation directions we included the information on product storage. Sara Lee's Coffee Cake was ready for in-store test marketing in several regions of the country. (Lucky consumers!)

Early on I was impressed by how well-organized the department was, how consistently the special skills and talents of each staff member were utilized. Miss Latzke was an educator at heart and welcomed the opportunity to share her knowledge. She'd encourage staff members to venture beyond their accredited talents and skills. She took her position seriously, as she did the positions and futures of her staff. Never was she too busy to discuss an idea or a problem with you. Feminine to her fingertips, she managed with a velvet glove, but with consistency and integrity you could rely on.

We collaborated with the Dairy and Poultry Department on many projects. "Pan o' Gold Chicken" was also designed for the burgeoning frozen food market. A frying chicken, weighing about three pounds, was cut up; each piece dipped in melted butter and then rolled in crushed, seasoned Pepperidge Farm bread crumbs, and placed in a rectangular foil pan. It was lightly drizzled with a little more golden melted butter, covered and consigned to the freezer. There it "roosted" until removed and, still frozen, baked in a hot oven for about an hour. A time and work-saver to build a light, or a many-course, meal around.

Armour's Frozen Stuffed Turkeys were another welcome addition to the poultry section of the market. Of necessity, to avoid possible bacterial problems, the stuffed turkeys had to fly a nonstop route from freezer to hot, hot oven, for a brief "delay en route." The consumer would brush hot melted butter or margarine over the ice-cold bird. That step resulted in a congealed coat of armor which, although it melted quickly, generated a very objectionable smoky haze in the test kitchen. So much testing, retesting—and turkey-tasting—went into the development of a fail-proof method of baking that would produce a tender, succulent bird in a reasonable baking time. And, of course, without the smoky haze prelude. We had succeeded in our goal of easing, for many homemakers, the then once-or-twice-a-year challenge of preparing Thanksgiving and Christmas dinners.

A new emphasis in the D and P Department's activities was prompted by consistent increases in sales of their cheese line. John Drain, a recent addition to the department, was appointed district manager of sales. An earnest young man with a verifiable Southern drawl and politeness, he was an idea man, and found our department staff an ideal sounding board. One morning he came by to see me and, over a cup of coffee, we discussed the sales potential of packaged shredded cheese. I "listened with all my ears," but my enthusiasm for the idea failed to match John's. Growing up I'd been at home in our kitchen from childhood, and having majored in Food and Nutrition and loving cheese myself, I'd never viewed grating or shredding it as a challenging chore. More problematic would be production and storage of the shredded product, the bacterial and mold hazards, and, of course, cost considerations. John had not ignored these factors, but he felt strongly that consumers hated shredding and inevitable finger-nicks or cuts, or broken nails. And the sticky shredder that was a pain to wash. His points were valid and he wanted to pursue the idea. He'd keep us posted.

Consumer interest in food and its preparation was accelerating. The realization that consumers welcomed products that were more table-ready, requiring less preparation time, affected the entire food industry. The wartime and post-war exodus of many women from the kitchen to jobs outside the home enabled them to pay for the convenience of these products.

Something big—like Julia Child—was happening in television. Food shows were popping up all over the horizon. My "premier" food-related TV appearance was linked to a mid-fifties heart attack suffered by the then President Dwight Eisenhower. His extended hospitalization taxed the media's efforts to provide fresh daily reports on his condition. When the President commented on how he was enjoying the new "Beef Bacon" and was pleased that it was allowed on his low-cholesterol diet, the comment was front-page, prime-time news. This Armour product, made from meat covering "plate" ribs of beef rather than pork ribs, was leaner than traditional bacon. Our Beef Department welcomed a call from the CBS-Chicago affiliate inviting an Armour representative to appear on their Clint Youle Weather segment. It was transmitted nightly to the Huntley-Brinkley Evening News originating in New York. So Beef Department head Frank Tobin and I, equipped with product samples to show—and an electric skillet—headed for the CBS studio in the Merchandise Mart. Frying the Breakfast Beef on camera, I provided the characteristic breakfast time sizzle for viewers. If only we could have transmitted the characteristic breakfast-time aroma too!

Food company program representatives were being invited to schedule TV appearances. Quality of the shows varied, as did the caliber of the studio "kitchens." To describe some of them as under-equipped would be an understatement. Our regular program staffers, Betty Cook in New York, Jeanne Bryant in the Midwest area, Ruth Klumb on the West Coast, and Virginia Moore in Birmingham, quickly learned the art of improvising.

Although programming was not a standard part of my job description, I did appear a number of times on the very popular weekly "Breta

Griem Show" in nearby Milwaukee. Breta was instantly credible, a mature woman who knew food and identified with the way Milwaukee-area homemakers cooked—long on butter, eggs, whipped cream and sour cream. Her wavy white hair, nicely styled, and her smiling blue eyes made her a TV natural.

She was open and conversational with her viewers, as though she were a favorite neighbor dropping by. After she identified and gave a warm welcome to her guest, Breta would turn over almost the entire program time to her, but Breta was always available to assist in any way. The 10 A.M. timing of the show required going to Milwaukee the day before the program, first to touch base with Breta, then to shop for groceries and spend the afternoon in the studio on pre-preparation. Whether a large ham or a leg of lamb was to be the star of my Easter-time presentation, several stand-ins of the product, at different stages of preparation were needed. And I planned to demonstrate on camera the preparation of a few dishes to round out the menu: an appetizing vegetable or two, a crisp salad, a picture-pretty dessert. After the program wind-up, a chat with Breta and, often the scheduling of a return appearance, it was back to Chicago.

For several months now, the rumor mill had been on fine grind, with any number of versions of "the company's imminent move from Chicago." But to <u>where</u>? And how would a move affect our Consumer Service Department? Finally the word came from the top: the general office would be moving into the relatively new Sun-Times Building, just off Michigan Avenue and close to the Wrigley Building. Our department would occupy offices and a new consumer test kitchen on the very top floor overlooking the Chicago River. Planning began immediately, and somehow the move was not too complicated. As one staff member who grew up in rural Iowa observed, "We're like farm women coming into town with the egg money."

In the midst of all this excitement, I was caught up in helping my family plan a late June Golden Wedding celebration for our parents in Dubuque.

Central to the celebration was a Mass in the Cathedral offered by Father Loras, at which Mother and Dad repeated their 1908 wedding vows. A surprise feature of the beautiful Mass was the unrestrained bell-ringing at prescribed and unprescribed times. Loras had given

David and Billy, young sons of my brothers John and Bill, a crash-course in altar-boying and they seemed to sense what a joyous occasion this was. They were eager to contribute!

After Mass the gathering shifted to nearby Farley, Iowa at the home of my sister Helen and her husband, Gene Willis, for a typical "Willis feast" on their velvety-green back yard. I watched the joyous intermingling of the young cousins, Bill's two from California, John's four from Wisconsin, and Mary's two from Illinois. Family bonding, I mused, may become more difficult in our increasingly mobile society. But when distances are dissolved and schedules rearranged, it is more than worth the effort.

1958-1963

It was a long train ride. But then it had been a long weekend, too. Father Loras had driven into Long Island from his parish in Delhi, Iowa to visit Mary's family and several New York friends. When he began having severe headaches and difficulty speaking, he was admitted to St. Vincent's Hospital. He lapsed into a coma which added to difficulties in diagnosis. He remained comatose for nearly a week before, on Friday, he took a turn for the worse. I was able to book an a.m. Saturday flight from O'Hare, to be with him and the Walshes. They'd been on watch the entire week, keeping us all posted daily. We ate a light supper before driving to St. Vincent's.

Christopher was not yet 4, Mary Elizabeth, just 1. Little Chris understood that Uncle Loras was in the hospital but seemed to sense that something was different, and very sad. He burst into tears but calmed down when told that Mrs. Feldman, a compassionate, toddler-friendly neighbor, would stay with them until we returned.

Little Christopher's uncle was still comatose, unaware that we were there. He had had a tracheotomy a day or so before and was restless, agitated. But <u>we</u> knew, and we felt blessed to share these last hours of his short 46 years of life.

Making funeral arrangements on a Sunday was challenging. Many details had to wait for Monday. There was space available for all five of us on an early-a.m. flight to Chicago on Tuesday. However, the small Ozark plane connecting us to Dubuque could not accommodate the coffin carrying Father Loras's body. It had to be transported by rail. The "Land of Corn" originated in Chicago's Illinois Central station on 11th and Michigan and would arrive in Dubuque around 8 p.m. Tuesday. Clearly, it would be wiser for Mary, Noel and the little ones to go ahead on Ozark and get to Dubuque as soon as possible. I'd wait for the later Land of Corn departure. It was a long wait and a long train ride until I was met on the front porch by my heart-broken Mom and Dad and family.

Father Loras's parishioners, shocked and saddened by the death of their pastor, so wanted to have a visitation and funeral liturgy in the church that he and they loved. It was a beautiful farewell from his mainly rural flock. A second funeral Mass took place in the Cathedral of St. Raphael, where Loras was baptized, made his First Communion, was confirmed and ordained. The church attended by his immigrant grandparents, Michael and Mary Sullivan, in the mid-to late 1800s. The Mass was on a bright, cloudless Saturday morning, one month to the day since our family had gathered in the Cathedral for Mother and Dad's joyous Golden Jubilee celebration.

Returning to Chicago by Zephyr on Sunday, the day after the Cathedral funeral, allowed precious meditating time. My thank-you list was lengthy. At the top, gratitude to God for sparing my dedicated, purpose-driven brother, a remaining life of total disability. To Mom and Dad and the family for their resignation to losing Loras. To the medical community, the funeral facilitators, to Armour for their sympathy and generosity, and for the many expressions of sympathy we received. Not least of all, on my arrival in Chicago, and entering the cavernous Union Station, for the loyal friends waiting to take me home.

Back at work on Monday, I welcomed a catch-up report on the week away and a busy schedule for the months ahead. A film on consumer frozen foods which had been in the planning stages for several months, was ready for production. Miss Latzke, Virginia Ames, our Food Service home economist, and I, together with the company's audio-visual director and the Frozen Foods Department manager constituted the Armour creative crew that "went Hollywood."

The film production process was fascinating! An absorbing lesson in the successful melding together of the talent and training backgrounds of all involved. It was made even more interesting when we were told that actor Ernest Borgnine was working on TREET commercials on the set next to ours. (TREET was Armour's competitor to Hormel's SPAM.) Borgnine wanted to meet the "Armour folks."

He was so "himself" and unassuming. Easy to talk with. He had just been nominated for an Oscar for his role in "Marty." "I'll never win the award, of course, but it's a thrill just to be nominated." In the low-budget movie he plays a 34-year old butcher who has next to no confidence in himself and fears he'll NEVER find romance. But he meets a young woman at a dance who feels the same way about herself. They click and the Oscar is his. He enlivened TV during the sixties when he starred in the comedy show "McHale's Navy."

Shortly before joining Armour, I had signed up for some writing classes at Northwestern University's Evening School on Chicago Avenue, not far from the Loop. The Medill School of Journalism was noted for shaping aspiring word-smiths into polished authors and journalists. Some of the instructors were connected with Chicago newspapers. Others, from a fascinating range of career paths. All had sold articles or stories to leading magazines. Women's magazines, which ran three or four short stories an issue, in addition to informative articles, provided a fertile market for writers in those early TV days. Both fiction and nonfiction writing classes were well-attended, by students who had been successful in publishing and those who were persevering. Later, because I fit into the former group, I was invited to be a member of the "Reading Team," entrusted with the evaluation/critiquing of students' writing efforts.

Prior to my Reading Team involvement, one of my short story efforts had survived the evaluation process and been given several good suggestions for making minor changes that would strengthen the story. Positive, encouraging comments, too. They spurred me on to re-read my story with more critical eyes, recognize and eliminate the flaws, and re-submit, hopefully to its previous reader. That happened. It came back promptly, with the reader's approval and the note, "Send it out!" Which I did. However, we were busier than ever at work, and on several projects entailing travel. The story was returned a month or so later in its toasty brown SASE and with a kindly rejection slip. I had scant time even to file it.

I did keep up with the Reading Team activity and learned a lot from it. One of the other members and I had become good friends and decided to sign up for the Nonfiction Writing Class taught by Lloyd Wendt, a Chicago Tribune editor. Mr. Wendt's latest book, *Give the*

Lady What She Wants, written with Herman Kogen, a Chicago Daily News editor, had appeared in the early '50s. It blends Marshall Field's retailing philosophy with early Chicago history. A generous number of charming etchings enrich the story. It's a great read, especially for Chicagoans and the innumerable visitors who put shopping at Field's at the top of their "To Do" lists. Unless travel pre-empted, neither Dick nor I would miss Mr. Wendt's class. A model teacher, he was in love with words and their usage, always enlivening the story.

Dick, by happenstance, was also a Grant Wood fan, and was interested in my connection with Stone City. For Christmas that year, he surprised me with a large framed print of Wood's "The Midnight Ride of Paul Revere," a favorite of mine. The model for Mr. Revere's mount was a rocking-horse from the attic of a friend of Wood's. The white Colonial-style church which horse and rider are racing by take me back to the Catholic church where Father Loras offered Mass on so many happy weekends.

I recall so well our taking Christopher and Mary Elizabeth to brunch in the store's elegant Walnut Room during the Christmas holidays. (Baby Kathy, born on 1958 New Year's week-end, was happy at home under the loving care of their dear neighbor, Jo Feldman.) The beautifully decorated tree was sequoia-tall but with its fragrant branches reaching out to hug its delighted guests. A dietitian friend of mine was in charge of menu-planning for the Walnut Room. She was endowed with creative genes, creative ideas that were production-practical. The children decided to skip their snap-crackle-pop rice krispies that day! The children's menu was tailored to the many wide-eyed youngsters. Who wouldn't be eager to try "Aunt Holly's Scrambled Eggs" with Sausage Bits, with Reindeer Toast on the side?

Order-taking was done by Mama as she trained each of us to <u>do it well</u>!

We loved Aunt Kate's tales of staying out of school every Spring to take new little goslings to pasture every day

Cousin Catharine was so good about taking us to the library. We thought it was a Temple of Wonders!

*First four Holmberg children;
In back, Loras and Bill. In front,
Helen and Rita*

*Papa's business was doing well. Then
along came The Great Depression . . .*

What a heady experience, that trip with the Berwangers was! (Even though I was perhaps the most "football uninformed" in Soldier Field.)

The newly ordained Father Loras serving mainly first in rural parishes and sharing his love of the land with his people, got to work on another priority, helping me to pursue a college degree.

A weekly radio food and nutrition program which had an enthusiastic studio audience and a very long run.

The big day when the students open the sealed envelopes that disclose the appointments or non-appointments to the hospital dietetic internships they've applied for.

Our duty uniforms were narrow—striped toasty brown and white seersucker. Dress uniform for off-duty drive into the Smokies.

V-mail from younger brother, John, from somewhere in the European Theater or in North Africa, where he served combat for four years.

Picture accompanied my reportage, as well as going with my first sale of a short story.

Mary's wedding with our family attending. In back: John, his wife Lucille, and Bill. In front: Helen, Maid of honor Rita, Noel and Mary, Mother, Dad and Father Loras.

Held in a south-of-town area, mindful of Ireland's Wicklow Hills close to Dublin, Helen's reception must have seemed a pretty formal occasion for niece Joan Holmberg, 8, and brothers David, 6, and Michael, almost 3. Tearful little Christopher Walsh, displaying for him, a totally unexpected reaction.

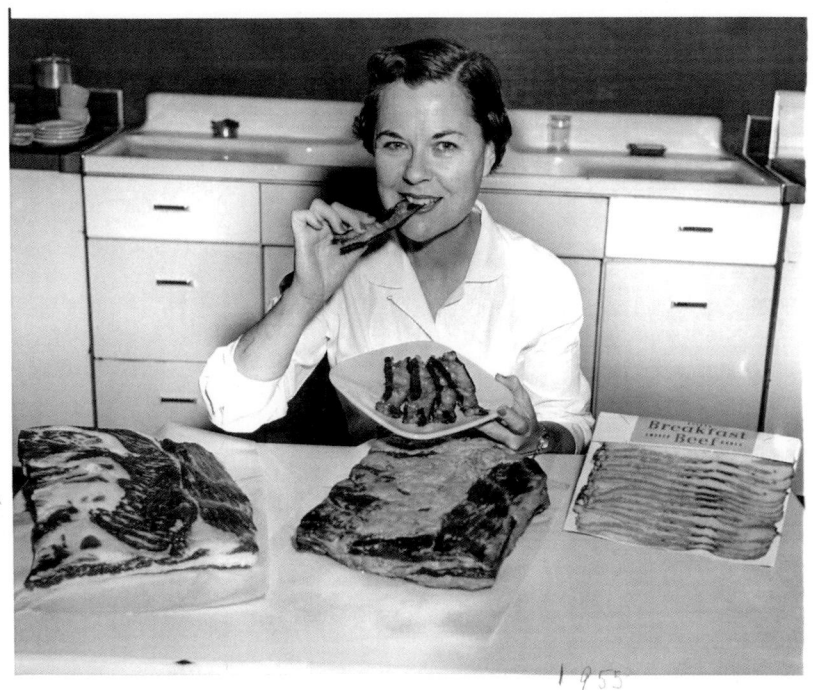

President Eisenhower's appreciation of the new Armour product, Beef Bacon, was a welcome news angle for reporters covering his story.

ACADEMY AWARD winner, Ernest Borgnine, was making Treet commercials at the same studio when this group of Armour people arrived in Hollywood to make a consumer frozen foods film for the Company.

The group got together for this picture. L. to r., C. N. Shaw, Mr. Borgnine, Rita Holmberg, Donald Lane, Stanley Neal Productions; Esther Latzke, Virginia Ames and Ralph Parks.

Ernest Borgnine was 99 44/100% natural in Hollywood's reach for sophistication and swagger.

1908 wedding of author's parents. With the hat the dear bride wore, who needed a flower girl?

The Golden Jubilarians both enjoyed every moment of the day.

THE ARMOUR MAGAZINE

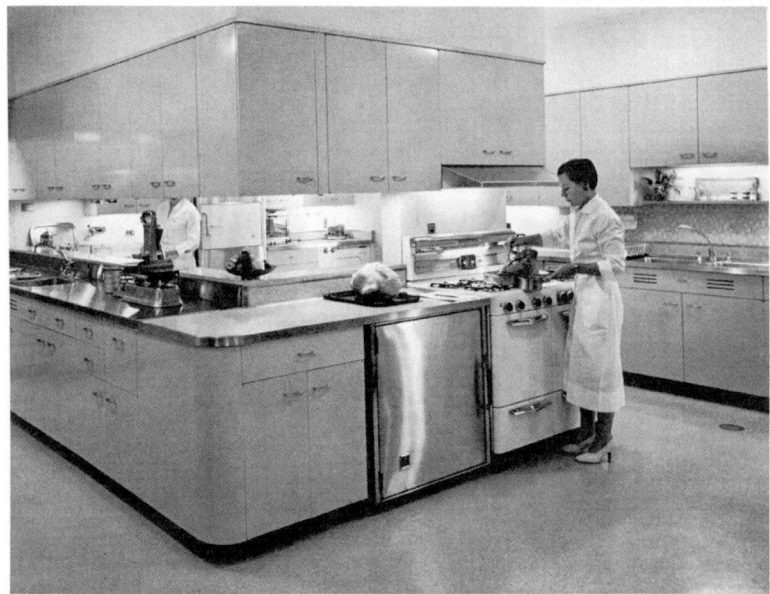

PLENTY of working space is one feature of new Armour consumer kitchens. Here Rita Holmberg, assistant director, roasts a turkey quarter.

Quite a contrast to our Stock Yards Test Kitchen.

Publicity photo for my new challenges at McCann-Erickson after leaving Armour.

double p-nutty cookies
(Super-crisp — peanut brittle fans take note!)

½ cup Peter Pan Smooth or Crunchy Peanut Butter
½ cup butter
1½ cups firmly packed brown sugar
¼ cup granulated sugar
2 eggs
3 cups sifted all-purpose flour
1 teaspoon soda
1 cup shredded coconut
1 cup salted Spanish peanuts, whole ("red-skins")

Cream together peanut butter and butter. Add sugars gradually and cream together until light and fluffy. Add eggs and vanilla and beat well. Mix in flour sifted together with soda. Stir in coconut and peanuts. Drop from spoon onto lightly greased cooky sheet and flatten down with a fork. Bake in moderate oven (375°F.) for about 15 minutes. Makes 6 dozen cookies.

molasses cookies
(Soft, plump cookies studded with raisins and with the flavor of old-fashioned molasses chip candy.)

½ cup Peter Pan Smooth or Crunchy Peanut Butter
¼ cup butter
¼ cup firmly packed brown sugar
½ cup molasses
1 egg
1 teaspoon vanilla
1 cup sifted all-purpose flour
½ teaspoon salt
1 teaspoon baking powder
½ teaspoon soda
1 cup raisins (or chopped dates)

Cream together peanut butter and butter. Add sugar and molasses and cream together until light and fluffy. Add egg and vanilla and beat well. Mix in dry ingredients, which have been sifted together, and then stir in raisins. Chill dough slightly. Then drop by teaspoonfuls onto lightly greased cooky sheet. Bake in moderate oven (375°F.) for 10 to 12 minutes. Makes about 4 dozen cookies.

oatmeal refrigerator cookies
(Good "make-ahead, bake-later" cookies!)

½ cup Peter Pan Smooth or Crunchy Peanut Butter
½ cup butter
2 cups firmly packed brown sugar
1 teaspoon vanilla
2 eggs
1¾ cups sifted all-purpose flour
2 teaspoons soda
¾ teaspoon salt
1½ cups rolled oats
½ cup chopped nuts

Cream together peanut butter and butter. Add sugar gradually and cream together until light and fluffy. Add vanilla and eggs and beat well. Mix in flour sifted together with soda, salt and vanilla. Then add rolled oats and nuts and shape dough into rolls about 2 inches in diameter. Wrap in waxed paper or plastic food wrap and chill in refrigerator. Slice about ¼ inch thick, place on cooky sheet and bake in moderate oven (350°F.) about 15 minutes. Makes 6 to 6½ dozen cookies.

(The rolls of dough may be kept in the refrigerator for 3 or 4 days and sliced and baked as needed.)

toffee bars
(Attractive, scrumptious-tasting — a "super" all the way!)

1 cup Peter Pan Smooth or Crunchy Peanut Butter (divided)
½ cup butter
1 cup firmly packed brown sugar
1 teaspoon vanilla
2 cups sifted all-purpose flour
¼ teaspoon salt
1 (6-oz.) package semi-sweet chocolate pieces, melted

Cream together ½ cup of the peanut butter and the butter. Add sugar gradually and cream together until light and fluffy. Beat in egg and vanilla. Mix in flour sifted together with salt. Spread dough on ungreased cooky sheet about 14 x 17 inches. Bake in slow oven (325°F.) for 20 to 25 minutes. Blend remaining ½ cup of peanut butter with the melted chocolate and spread mixture on cooky surface. Cut into diamonds while still warm. Garnish each diamond with whole or chopped peanuts, if desired. Makes about 4 dozen Toffee Bars.

2-way Peter Pan discs
(Crisp, flavorful — be ready to make them again and again!)

½ cup Peter Pan Smooth or Crunchy Peanut Butter
1 cup butter
½ cup granulated sugar
1 cup firmly packed brown sugar
1 egg
1 teaspoon vanilla
1½ cups sifted all-purpose flour
¼ teaspoon salt
1 teaspoon cinnamon
¼ cup chopped nuts
Shredded coconut

Cream together peanut butter and butter. Add sugar gradually and cream together until light and fluffy. Beat in egg and vanilla. Mix in flour sifted together with salt. Chill dough slightly. Shape into small balls. Roll half the balls in mixture of cinnamon and nuts. Roll remaining balls in shredded coconut. Place about 2 inches apart on cooky sheet and bake in moderate oven (375°F.) about 15 minutes. Makes about 5 dozen cookies.

Completed Peter Pan collection of recipes starring an ingredient that's a family favorite.

It's coming Sunday, October 26...
The best of 20 years of Recipe Roundup

100 recipes as selected by Rita Holmberg, noted food preparation expert and former food editor of Better Homes & Gardens magazine.

Many readers in the area have saved the Roundup food sections for the entire two decades

Dubuquer's breads 'sweet as a bakery's'

Baking sweet breads "as tempting as any in a bakeshop window" is easy when you follow Dubuquer **Rita Holmberg's** instructions in her latest article in the April 24 issue of Woman's Day, which is on magazine racks now.

Holmberg develops all her recipes from scratch and then tests and retests them.

Holmberg, a part-time instructor in foods and nutrition at Clarke College and author of a cookbook entitled "Great Dishes from the Oven," has written several articles about food and nutrition for magazines such as Woman's Day, Family Circle and Bon Appetit, as well as trade magazines.

Also a dietetics and consumer information consultant for several large Midwestern corporations, she still finds time to sew, knit, travel and go cross-country skiing.

Holmberg

Elise applied the book's content to an article on baking your own Sweet Breads I'd had published about that time in Woman's Day.

It has many worthwhile ideas, such as preparing two oven meals at once, one for baking it today, the other to tuck in the freezer, to bake later.

It's always rewarding to receive appreciative comments on the text from an instructor. And especially, occasional comments from students.

The Creamery itself is enhanced by an excellent restaurant, a cheese-wine store and an interesting gift shop.

After giving his mother his priestly blessing, they share a special joy.

The newly ordained Father Chris blessed "Tante Rita," his Godmother, with Aunt Helen alongside.

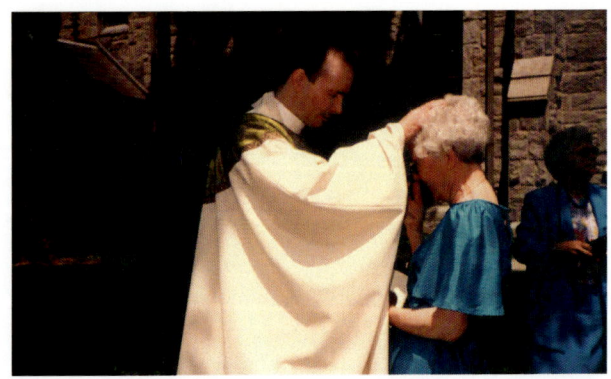

Father Chris with Rita and Kathy's husband, Jim waiting.

Mary and Julie walk among mid-summer's flowers at Hancock Shaker Museum.

Rita, exploring the weaving skills of the loom.

"Back at the House," Julie, Father Chris, Aunt Rita, with Michael offside, resting before Mass on the deck and before Michael's White Lasagna supper.

Kathy, Jim and their "Four Little Women" came for the day.

"Mountaineering"—focusing the telescopic view of the world below. A stop for early supper at a charming family restaurant.

Uncle Chris and pre-teen Mary Kate having a chat before the weary mountaineers head for home.

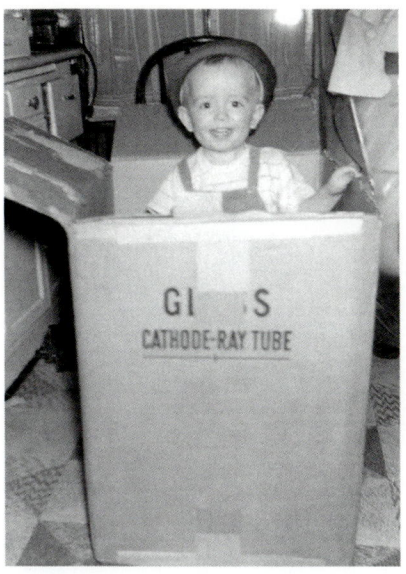

Toddler Chris at about two, jubilant in an emptied shipping carton

Later, somewhere on the road to 50—always animated.

Right: *Ann and Michael's trio: Caley, Meghan and Connor. When a little older, and with a new little brother, Patrick, the quartet were gift-bearers at Devotions in the Sister's chapel before Uncle Chris's 50th birthday reception. Fully costumed so they could go on to trick-or-treating.*

Aunt Rita, Mary, Father Chris with a few of the Brigittine sisters, and a gentleman Retreat House resident.

Sunday evening's Orientation Dinner at the Dubuque Fairgrounds. Monday's obviously carefully planned program was explained in detail. And it would be beautifully expedited by friendly Honor Flight folks. The evening made the prospect of the next morning's pre-dawn sign-in less difficult.

A group similar to this one welcomed us at every planned stop, as well as on our late return to Dubuque.

As former teachers, we were impressed by what carefully researched material was presented at each memorial we visited.

As the only female WWII veteran in our group that day, I was invited with Perry Mason, to place the ceremonial wreath on the memorial.

How did we ever deserve such an ideal day for our Honor Flight!

Vets on the Dubuque Honor flight included many from the Korean Conflict and Viet Nam, as well as from a dwindling number of World War II vets. At the last memorial this group snap was taken. (Capless Lt. Rita Holmberg was in the irregular rear row, to the right of the vet at the end of the row facing camera.)

The Viet Nam Memorial may be the most photographed of all six which we viewed that day. Here, a few of my fellow-vets, with me and my guardian Barb, shared its historic impact.

What a fitting close to our day of viewing these touching War Memorials!

Covert operators Father Chris and Michael Walsh, with Aunt Rita, on Friday evening at "Il Palio", an exceptionally fine restaurant. Keeping Barb and me under wraps was vital!

On Saturday P.J. Hoyt, "G-Mom's" grandson, greeting Aunt Rita at the Parish Center a half hour before the birthday bell, as commanded.

Planned—and actualized—by Kathy, with help from her four enthusiastic daughters.

Small wonder that Father Chris and his Mom are beaming.

Michael Walsh, Mary Hoyt, Kathy Alber, Ann Henderson, Father Chris Walsh, Mass celebrant, the birthday Mom and her sister Rita.

1963-1968

Summertime in Chicago offered numerous opportunities for free time activities. Although the Stock yards-to-Loop move in 1958 had been achieved, some changes in Consumer Service Department routines were in order.

In the Yards, the General Office Building across the street from us included a retail market. They supplied us with meat and poultry items as ordered for product testing and recipe development. "Jim," a mild-mannered, middle-aged black man, our "porter," would pick up the order and deliver it to the Test Kitchen. One of the home economists would go shopping on a regular schedule at a nearby supermarket for basic and specific food items. Without fail, Jim would be "at the ready" to unload the station wagon. He was as reliable as Lake Michigan's breezes. We all recognized that if a staff member were traveling or absent for any other reason, she wouldn't be missed half as much as if Jim were a "no-show." Had Jim gone beyond third or fourth grade or had he even started school? When one day he was helping me store an assortment of photo props, I was called to the phone. Handing him the bright red marker, I asked him if he'd please mark the end of the box "Odds and Ends"? On my return, he'd done that and placed the box on the shelf. In bright scarlet the identification "ODZ AN INZ."

In our heart-of the-Loop location, food procurement was a bit more complex until home economist Ruth Rust volunteered a solution. She lived on the near North side and would be able to shop early at a supermarket near her apartment, walk the short distance with her bounty to the subway stop, get on board and head for the stop very close to the Sun-Times Building. It would require shorter shopping lists, more frequent trips and lighter loads, she pointed out. "But I grew up on a farm, I learned how to carry heavy loads," Ruth insisted. "And, first I'll eat a good breakfast to fortify myself!"

After Ruth's first trial run of her proposed plan, several of us helped her unpack. Somewhere between a stalk of bushy-topped celery and a large package of lamb chops, a soft squeal came from Mary Lou Culin, our newest staff member. "Ruth! What is that on your ring finger?" Surrounded right away by the rest of the staff, the rather shy Ruth showed us the beautiful diamond Jack Brown had given her the night before. She radiated happiness. A couple of the not-yet engaged quickly offered to take over the shopping responsibility if Ruth guaranteed such a joyous outcome.

Organizational changes at Armour were taking place also. Unexpectedly, after over three decades of heading the Consumer Service Department, Miss Latzke would be retiring early and a pleasant young man, said to have a marketing background, would become director in her place. (No direction was forthcoming from anyone on how or whether we would try to explain the "Marie Gifford" trade name with male directorship.) The uncertainty of the department's future prompted me to investigate two job offers, one local, the other in the East. However, I wasn't eager to leave Chicago. Now with close to a dozen years at Armour, I was still pleased with the way my job had developed into a mix of editorial responsibilities, new product development and promotional activities. Armour was a considerate, just employer, Miss Latzke a conscientious, wise mentor. Not least of all, there was the smooth-running Consumer Service Department, each member with clearly defined, but not limiting, responsibilities. Miss Latzke's legacy.

Often two home ec friends who also worked in the Loop, met me for lunch, sometimes at Stouffer's on Wabash, sometimes at the restaurant on the top floor of the lakeside Prudential Building. This day was special because Sophia Lovekamp had been on the staff of the National Live Stock and Meat Board and was soon to marry her minister-fiancé and move from Chicago. Helen Wolcott was Home Economist at McCann-Erickson Advertising's Chicago branch for a number of years and had recently accepted a position with Pillsbury in Minneapolis. She would be heading the Home Economics Department there and acquiring the trade name, "Ann Pillsbury." After a toast to the soon-to-be departers, we had much to discuss over lunch. I succeeded in avoiding any mention of my concerns. I had shared a few of them with Helen earlier. She said that she'd told the agency manager, Chet Posey, about me as a likely candidate for the McCann job.

His call came late that same day. Could I join him for lunch on Thursday? That was workable. So on Thursday noon I hopped on the bus to go the six or seven blocks between the Sun Times and the McCann office on South Michigan. We had a pleasant chat. ("Rita, my first name is "Chet," not "Mr. Posey") Then we walked in the brisk January air to the Palmer House Petite Café for lunch and job details. At that time the Agency's major food account was Swift and Company, with their established line of meats and poultry. Butterball Turkey had been introduced only recently and was taking center stage in the poultry market. One particular Butterball Turkey ad portraying an old-fashioned family offering grace before an old-fashioned Thanksgiving dinner, had become a classic.

Derby Foods was another account, the manufacturer of Peter Pan Peanut Butter and a line of canned meats. Another one was the Milk Foundation, a trade group. My meat and poultry experience at Armour would be considered an asset, particularly on the first two accounts. Also, I'd be expected to contribute ideas, in addition to checking the accuracy of copy relating to food and the validity of any claims made in copy. A good lunch, a good interview and an attractive job offer. I told Chet that I'd like a little pondering time but would get my decision to him by the beginning of the next week, if that was OK with him.

Early that evening I jotted down the pluses and minuses of the McCann job, as well as those in my changing Armour job. Then, while eating a light supper, I compared the two columns, weighed the situation, reached a decision, and went to bed early, so I wouldn't succumb to any mind-changing. I'd call Chet Posey on Monday, to say I'd accept the job.

Leaving Armour was cushioned by my plan to take a Deluxe Limousine tour of Mexico, originating in Mexico City and winding up in Cuernavaca. A Chicago friend who wanted to come along was unable to arrange the mid-winter get-away. But our 17-member tour group, in the main, was a very interesting, cordial blend, eager to explore the Mexico of the mid-1900's. The exception was a stocky, cigar-smoking man who resembled pictures of Napoleon. He was frequently observing, as we drove through the sunny country-side and up into the mountains, "This certainly ain't like Hawaii." He and Laura, his gracious wife, had toured the Islands the previous year. Unfortunately, Laura had a heart condition and couldn't take the high altitude as we rode further up into the mountains.

The relaxed, unhurried pace of life in Mexico, the sunshine and warmth were reflected in the Mexican people. In turn, I felt relaxed and enjoyed the leisurely limo rides through the small villages and towns like Guadalajara with its large University, and Cuernavaca, the popular, very attractive town for northern retirees to locate. With only four or five passengers to a limo, those rides were like enjoyable family drives. I regretted my inability to speak Spanish and to converse with the friendly people at the various places we visited. But I was familiar enough with French and the Latin liturgy, that I could often make connections—or guesses—with the Spanish language.

I was in awe and speechless, when we visited the Cathedral of Guadalupe and witnessed faith-filled peasants, on their knees, prayerfully approaching the church entrance across the large, wide plaza.

The time in Mexico whipped by. The return to Chicago was highlighted by an atypical detour to New York which, actually, was a well-planned delay enroute. Noel had been transferred to the New York office of the Irish tourist Board and the family, which now included three-year-old Ann Maureen, was living on Long Island. One of the first evenings of my stay she was "helping" me by setting the table for supper and asked if I would still be there the next day, "Yes, honey, I'm staying three more days, till Sunday." She smiled "I'm glad, Aunt Rita, because I like you. I really do." My quick reply: "I'm glad, Ann, because I like you, too. I love you!" She stood stock-still, a table knife in one hand, a spoon in the other. "Well, I love you so much, I wish you was in our family!" (She was learning the art of one-upmanship!)

Transition to the McCann-Erickson job was much simplified by the kitchen manager, Henrietta Knudson. A dear lady of Polish descent, in her 50's, and married to Elmer Knudson, a city bus driver, she had never worked outside their home before. She had a strong work ethic and found her job exciting. She also treated her "boss" as royalty. On my first day there, around 9 a.m., she appeared in my office with a tray holding a small pot of freshly brewed coffee and a toasty-warm Danish.

Working with a staff of eight to ten in the Armour Consumer Service Department compared to the new staff of "me and Henrietta" took some getting used to. However, the warm welcome extended by the copy chief and crew, the art director, the librarian, the entire agency, reassured me. Very important for me, Swift and company's Home Economics Department, headed by Jeanne Paris, another home ec friend, was probably equal in size to Armour's. Jeanne and her staff had worked well with Helen Wolcott and were pleased that I was filling the McCann job.

Although winter in Chicago was still with us, McCann's creative minds were, of course, in the "think ahead" mode. Summertime with its cookouts, picnics and hot weather meals. Autumn, with back-to-school and outdoor activities that increase appetites, tailgate parties and more indoor entertaining. Great opportunities for selling their clients' products through attention-getting, realistic ads. Everyone was working on a fast track.

A Derby Foods project, the production of a "Peter Pan Cookbook," actually a soft-cover booklet, became a popular joint agency effort, especially during the recipe testing and tasting stages. The peanut-buttery aromas wafting down through the hallways from Henrietta's kitchen became a magnetic force. We had no problems whatsoever in recruiting tasters. Project manager was an experienced, creative copy-writer, with a lively interest in food and cooking. As we generated ideas on the book's content, we discussed them with the designer, a budding young artist with rather a limited food experience, but with an eagerness to learn. When we ran the gamut—appetizers, breads, cakes and frostings, confections, cookies, pastries, sauces, sandwiches, and puddings and other desserts—he credited us with legerdemain! He came up with an innovative concept of alternating the pages, white and peanut-butter colored. Scattered throughout were drawings of the finished foods of each chapter. When the book was opened, its front and back covers formed a double-spread with an array of the peanut butter goodies made from the recipes inside.

The Milk Foundation account was handled by Jeff, perhaps in his mid-30's, the father of three girls, who pleasantly surprised me with his understanding of basic nutrition principles. He had a couple of concepts which he felt had potential and wanted to get my thoughts on them. One was to confront the "thin-ness" goal of so many young girls and women in our society today, almost to the point of anorexia. Normally, at these ages, they are disinterested in health warnings. They feel invincible. If indeed, they are anorexics, they consider themselves FAT, regardless of successful pound-shedding.

Jeff and I certainly recognized thinness to the point of skinniness as a serious health problem. We were also cognizant of how difficult it would be to tackle, in either print or television ads. In the advertising field, he had earned laurels for his creativity in converting serious subject matter into simple, understandable form. He had the "light touch," but never at the sacrifice of well-researched information. I shared with Jeff some of my file material on eating disorders and suggested a couple of excellent references he could contact for fresh, reliable research data. It was encouraging to see someone so fired up on a project. "Maybe that's because I have a vested interest! Our twins are racing into their teens. They're starting to be fashion-and-fad conscious." We agreed on a catch-up meeting for a month later.

As I circled the date and time on my desk calendar, one of my parents' repeated bromides flashed through my mind: "The older we get, the faster the time goes!" How unobserving, I thought. They just don't understand. You wait for weeks for Easter and then for vacation to begin, and later, for Christmas and forever for your birthday. Now that I was in my forties, my parent's view on time's passage struck me as being quite perceptive.

A week or so before my birthday, I had a surprise phone call from Myrna Johnston, food editor of Better Homes and Gardens. She was in Chicago working on food photographs. She'd be returning to her Des Moines office at week's end. Could we meet for lunch the next day? Although I'd known Myrna for over two decades, mainly through professional and occasional social encounters, we weren't on the meeting-for-lunch circuit. The Drake Hotel, where she was staying, was near the photographer's studio, so we ate in one of my favorite eateries, the Cape Cod Room.

The photo shoot was wrapped up, and Myrna was delighted to have a free afternoon, maybe with time afterward to shop at Field's. Several mutual friends were living in Des Moines, so Myrna filled me in on them as well as on happenings with home ec associates. We'd both enjoyed the Baked Salmon Caesar Salad and the crusty little rolls that are in themselves a reason to eat in the Cape Cod Room. Fresh lime sherbet, sugar wafer implanted atop, for dessert. Over coffee, Myrna disclosed the motivation behind our cold mid-winter get-together. In another year, after thirty-five years as food editor of Better Homes, she would be retiring. Both she and the management, Meredith Publishing, with several Navy veterans among them, had decided that "getting a first assistant aboard" would ease Myrna's planned retirement. It would also facilitate the assistant's assumption of the food editor's job.

Part of the plan was for me to fly out to Des Moines soon for a couple of days to meet management staff and visit with the editorial and test kitchen staffs. I had mentioned that if a Thursday-Friday visit would be workable, I'd like to connect with a flight up to Dubuque to spend the weekend with my parents. Mother, confined to a wheelchair, and my dear care-giver father were in their late 80's. We settled on a late January date, but Ozark's Des Moines to Dubuque flight schedule for Saturdays offered little or no choice. We settled on making the short flight in a small Meredith plane on an early Saturday morning. A short passenger list, too: the magazine's executive editor, James Autry, and his 5-year old son, Jimmy, who sat in the window seat right next to me. When aloft, I pointed out to him a small number of cattle gathered near a barn. He hesitated, then said: "I can't see them, but I do see a chicken down there!"

Decision-making on the Better Homes opportunity was less difficult than on the break with Armour had been. There'd be the generation of ideas for food stories, the researching and investigation of new foods and food products, as well as the searching for interesting restaurants and novel eateries. More travel, which appealed to me. Most of the magazine's color photography was done in Chicago, New York, Los Angeles or San Francisco, and occasionally, on location. Not least important, I'd be writing and editing. I accepted the job in early March.

However since I faced uprooting from fourteen years in Chicago, finding housing in Des Moines and enduring the traumatic process of moving, I expected that I'd be ready to start by May 1st.

That year in the Midwest, Spring did arrive on schedule and exceeded its usual beauty. I was settled into an attractive, roomy apartment not too far from the magazine. Initiation into the new job was graciously handled. Before long I was submerged into a hefty stack of articles awaiting editing. Also, I was becoming accustomed to the twice-a-day "taste table" routine. Early in the morning and right after lunch, a test kitchen home economist would drop on the desks of each home economist on the editorial staff a listing of the recipes tested and to be tasted that morning or afternoon. Taste Table was at 10:30 a.m. and at 3 p.m. Discerning evaluation was not requested, but was required. All recipes had to be unanimously approved of to appear in the magazine or in a BHG cookbook.

Myrna continued full-time as food editor, of course. Prior to her retirement in Spring of 1965, she visited Hancock Village, a Shaker community set in the Berkshire Mountains of western Massachusetts. The Shakers were founded as an off-shoot of a Quaker community and were based on faith in God, simple living and hard work. Their celibate lifestyle resulted in dwindling membership. Hancock Village, in fact, was one of a very few remaining communities. On her return to the office, she placed several files bulging with information on my desk, telling me to write the story. Brochures, snapshots, scribbled-down recipes, notes on Shaker history to decode and verify. As the Shaker recipes were routed through the test kitchen and Taste Table process, they won unanimous approval, usually on the first run. Baked Apples in Cider, Maple Baked Squash, Mother Ann's Birthday Cake and many others.

For years, a gathering of food editors, home economists in business and related positions met in New York in early November to assess the many advances and changes being made in our food supply. Myrna and I had both attended and felt the meeting very worthwhile. We'd have time to prop-shop at a few favorite kitchen and tableware shops before returning to the Waldorf, where we were staying. We had planned to meet friends for dinner. It was only 4:30, already dusk, and we were cold and weary. So we stopped in Peacock Alley off the lobby, and ordered coffee and a few cookies to tide us over. No sooner than we'd nibbled on shortbread with our coffee than we were suddenly in total darkness! The hotel would be prepared, we assumed, to handle a brief electric system problem. We were all supplied with candles and flashlights, and at first almost enjoyed the Mardi Gras or New Year's Eve atmosphere. Waiters served soft ice cream from non-functioning freezers, with rapidly cooling coffee.

After a couple of hours, however, the frivolity mood changed. And the rumor-mill and conjecturing began. "It's a power failure." "It's affecting the entire North Atlantic coastal states." "It could be a nuclear attack." We were concerned about the friends we were to meet for dinner—<u>and</u> how, without elevator power we'd ever make it up to our rooms? Myrna was on the 16th floor, I was on the 8th. But make it we did, slowly and with frequent stairway stops. Power was not restored for two days. The hotel did an amazing feat of adapting to a scary emergency situation.

1968-1973

Another decade about to turn! Of late, that seemed to be happening at surprisingly rapid pace. The process of pulling together the food section of Better Homes and Gardens a dozen times a year required careful scheduling and ongoing attention to the calendar. Issue-planning meetings were held an entire year ahead of an issue's appearance in the reader's home. Photo shoots were set six months ahead. This meant, of course, that we would be doing photographs for the June issue in December. Procuring summer fruits and vegetables at that time of year was made a great deal less of a problem thanks to the top-rated George de Gennaro studio and the existence of the Los Angeles Farmers' Market, with its bounty and variety of picture-perfect produce. They could transform the most "common, ordinary"—or elegant food setups into award-winning paintings. So, December shooting the June issue was scheduled for a week in sunny California. The amount of recipe testing required depended on the theme of the section and the "banked" recipes we held in reserve. The theme itself often inspired a rush of creative recipe development by the Test Kitchen staff and made Taste Table doubly interesting.

Composing or "styling" the photo set-up was the next step. Interesting props, appropriate to the food or foods being shot, but not overpowering or distracting from them were a given. All the preliminary preparation was rewarded when, after my return to Des Moines, the finished photos arrived and were so great that they made writing the lead story of the food section an unalloyed pleasure.

Press tours and press parties were a very effective method for food and food-related equipment manufacturers to transmit information on their products, "old favorites" and newly developed ones.

The gatherings were informative, our hosts welcomed the opportunity to interface directly with us on a casual basis, to answer any questions and consider any suggestions we might have for new products. Always enjoyable and a good way for us to mingle with our food editor colleagues from different regions of the country.

The Fish and Seafood Industry sponsored a tour of the Boston Area for a group of twelve food editors. Most of us were familiar with the area, I'd guess, but I doubt whether any of us had ever before been on a research vessel close to the Atlantic Ocean on Gloucester's shoreland. After a memorable "seafood-of-choice" luncheon, we boarded the vessel for "show-and-tell time." The Association's scientists and their crew, garbed in slickers and hip-high rubber waders, had lowered a large, very coarse net to the ocean floor and skillfully dragged it a little above the surface of the floor. Then they hoisted the net up to the ship's deck, opened it, and spread out the flip-flopping creatures of the deep. Almost all of them were unfamiliar to us, but each diverse occupant of the net was clearly defined by our fishermen. Defined—<u>and</u> lauded for its high nutritive value.

The contents of that net, they stressed, represented a sample of a vast, under-utilized food source for our nation, a situation they are striving to change. We went on to their nearby Irradiation Laboratory, where they shared with us results of irradiation tests and studies. They thanked us for being an effective pipeline for passing along helpful, accurate information for our readers and urged us to make them aware of the merits of a wider availability of fish and seafood in the near future.

The next day we went to the bogs—the cranberry bogs, that is—as guests of Ocean Spray Cranberries, a company located near Middleboro not far from Cape Cod Bay. In early colonial days, the ruby red berries were converted into a sauce to brighten the Thanksgiving feast. For many years the pilgrims and their off-spring strung the berries on long cords to use in decorating their Christmas trees. The berries are grown in swampy land close to the ocean. We watched the harvesters, shod in rubber boots, quickly pluck the berries, toss them into a hod each of them carries and then transfer them into a large bin at the edge of the bog. After a thorough washing and drying they're ready for packaging, some in clear see-through bags and some to be converted into whole or jellied cranberry sauce. Ever since canning methods were perfected, they're a favorite accompaniment to turkey and other poultry or meat meals year 'round.

California, the entire United States away from the Atlantic Ocean, was the destination of another press tour and, happily, scheduled in the middle of a mean Midwest winter. The Citrus Growers Association sponsored the tour and invited a group of food editors. We departed after five days there with a wealth of information. This included tested citrus recipes, with photos, updated data on nutrition and helpful purchasing tips. Naval oranges, temple oranges, tangerines, tangelos, petite clementines in great abundance. We toured several small citrus groves and learned about the planting, their growing stages, and their harvesting. Sunkist was a member of the Citrus growers and focused on lemons and limes. A colleague and director of the Sunkist Kitchens, Barbara Clinton, had invited us for a lovely tea, with spectacular little lemon tarts and an assortment of scrumptious cookies. The day before the Citrus Growers' tour ended, Sunset Magazine had held an open house at their beautiful headquarters in Menlo Park, on San Francisco Bay. The food editor, Genevieve Callahan, had been a staff member at Better Homes and Gardens some years before. After leaving BH&G she moved to California where she and a friend, Lou Richardson, also a former BH&G staff member were recruited as senior editors of Sunset, the high-quality food magazine. It took baby steps but quickly earned accolades for the freshness of ideas, the clarity and readability of its copy. With Lou Richardson, Gen had also authored the book, How to Write for Homemakers, which became a bible for college Home Economics majors. For her know-how, her eagerness to share that know-how, _and_ for her sincerity and grace, I considered Gen a first class role model.

Reality struck, not too painfully, when I celebrated my 50th birthday and things in my personal life were prompting me to do some reflecting. Again, employing my proven decision-making process, I weighed the pros and cons of several options, decided to resign from Better Homes and go the free-lance route: limited product testing, an emphasis on writing, and consulting. The latter, because of my R.D./Registered Dietitian certification might include occasional consultation in health care facilities. The free-lancing would allow me more latitude in scheduling and less time in extended travel.

One of my first free-lance jobs was a request from Amana Industries to develop a dozen or so recipes specifically designed for microwave preparation. They had recently introduced their Amana Radar Range and supplied me with one for my accepted task. I had had only scant experience with microwave magic and its limitations. However, with the clear information in their well-written Amana Use Booklet and the enthusiastic support of the Amana people, I was successful in meeting the challenge. Amana is close to Des Moines and several times during the project, some of the Amana staff had been eager to stop by for Taste Table duty.

Soon after completion of the Amana project, a phone call came from a Dr. John Nelson of the Peavey Company in Minneapolis, a long-time family-run milling firm. They were "ingredient suppliers," the main thrust of their business directed to food product manufacturers, especially bakery items, doughnuts and a line of commercial bakery mixes. They also marketed high-quality durum wheat flour for use in the manufacture of pasta and pasta-based products.

Dr. Nelson, a former General Mills employee, had joined Peavey as a vice president to spearhead the Company's decision to enter the consumer market, to target the large segment of customers who prepare meals in home kitchens daily. A modern, fully-equipped research center designed to help achieve their goals was being built in the Chaska area twenty-some miles southwest of Minneapolis and Dr. Nelson (call me "John", please) was pursuing its staffing. A mutual friend from my Armour days had told him of my background and possible interest in the job as head of Consumer Service at the Center. John said he'd be happy to drive down to Des Moines someday soon so we could have dinner and discuss things.

The next week he and Jim Swanson, also formerly with General Mills and recently signed on by Peavey, came along. Jim will head the Engineering Department at the new Center. Their joint enthusiasm for the new endeavor was refreshing. That enthusiasm carried over when after dinner we had coffee and dessert at my apartment. They spread out, on my large desk-top, blueprints, sketches, snapshots, even newspaper clippings about their rising structure in Chaska. It would have a test kitchen, a conference room where taste panels could be conducted and food photos shot, and a research-rich, food-focused library with a full-time librarian. Laboratories were to be in the center of the building, staff offices on the perimeter. A pilot plant would adjoin and be connected to the main building by an enclosed bridge which would house the Engineering Department. The plant would manufacture small-scale lots of new products ready for test markets. Occupancy for the Center was set for June, 1969, (weather permitting, of course) which allowed me time to consider another big decision.

Before he and Jim headed home, John suggested that I come up to Minneapolis some day soon "to survey the territory" and meet some of the Peavey people. I promised I would.

I'd been enjoying the free-lancing, even the element of surprise in the diversity of the projects that came my way. Although my house-bound Mom and Dad were faring very well, I welcomed being able to drive up to Dubuque regularly to spend time with them. Sensing my hesitation, Dr. Nelson was understanding. Promptly, he proposed a Peavey project that I could help them out on. They had been investigating the soaring snack market, many of the items flour-based, but lacked facilities for product testing and taste panel evaluation, inputs which I could provide them. As a solo product tester, taste panel organizer and manager, as well as the preparer and transmitter of data, I began occasionally to feel like a whirling dervish!

After completion of my work on the snack project, I sent John a report. It was precisely what they needed, he said. Now could I prepare samples of those snacks which we judged to have special consumer appeal and send them to them? Jim Swanson could convert them into formulas for commercial production and do some cost analysis.

Two weeks had elapsed since our Des Moines visit. John's urgency about recruiting his staff was certainly understandable. He had taken on a big challenge and needed a strong support team, in the planning stage as well as in the future. I should make every effort not to delay my decision, whether it be accept or decline.

The next week I flew up on an early flight for a packed interview-type visit. First, to the Peavey General Offices in the Flour exchange, then to their labs down on the Mississippi Riverfront. Jim Swanson joined us for a late lunch at a restaurant near the Flour

Exchange, and drove out with us to view the far-from-completed Research Center in Chaska. The day was cold but the sky was clear blue. Beautiful rolling hills, snow-covered now, where a century ago Native American Indians and Scandinavian and German immigrants struggled to survive and build a life. The Center was being built on a rise of land and will overlook Lake Hazeltine. The late afternoon sun was just setting as we dashed to the airport for my flight back to Des Moines. As I had promised John, I called him two or three days later that I could be ready to join his group in late May.

My move to the 10,000 Lakes state, and into an apartment in Edina, took place toward the end of May. The suburb is about 15 miles from downtown Minneapolis and the Flour Exchange, where I'd office for a short period before the Research Center was ready for occupancy.

The group had been working also on a wild rice project: the harvesting, processing and packaging of an excellent Minnesota variety of the grain. Consumer Service would be responsible for package information—preparation methods, cooking times and storage tips, as well as for providing fresh, appealing recipes. Important too was the tracking of what was happening with rice products in general: new products, product extensions, new preparation methods, innovative packaging. The top-quality Twin Cities supermarkets like Byerly's, Jeny's and Lunds, and a number of creative specialty shops were a joy to explore.

In early October, only four months into the new job, an unplanned intervention! A small lump in my left breast, which I knew demanded prompt checking. The problem: I was "physicianless." I hadn't had time to line up a doctor. However, thanks to dear local friends and my concerned Peavey associates, I was fortunate to have the Chief of Staff at St. Mary's Hospital in Minneapolis, Dr. Louis Courtney Culigan, perform a biopsy. Immediate pathology tests revealed "a very small but fast-growing tumor" and, with my pre-surgery signed authorization, he performed a radical left mastectomy. When he came early the next morning to check me, his report was positive. No chemotherapy or radiation needed. A week in the hospital (standard in the late sixties) followed by regular checkups. Then he gave me a broad smile that reminded me of

Barry Fitzgerald in the unforgettable movie, "Bells of St. Mary's." "I see you're from Dubuque? I was born in Garryowen." (The small, picturesque village south of Dubuque was settled by Irish immigrants in the mid-1860's and to this day has remained Irish to the bone.) He patted my arm. "We'll take good care of you." And they did, indeed.

On my return to the job in early November, I resumed work on the snack and the wild rice projects. Help was also needed with the numerous decisions involved in furnishing and decorating our beautiful new structure. Selections of chairs for offices and conference room—sturdy, attractive and comfortable. Large potted plants for the reception area, the conference room and the library, invincible plants which would thrive indoors.

Settling in took a little time and with the winter holidays ahead, and the busy shopping, decorating and social schedules, we delayed until April the Open House we had planned. Many, if not most, of the staff were hardened Minnesotans but patient with my uneasy relationship with winter driving. By late March, having adjusted to some degree, I drove up to Duluth, to appear on a local TV food show. A month or so later, built on that happy outcome, I drove to Stout College in Menomonie, Wisconsin, well known for its programs in Home Economics, to speak at a dinner to majors in the field.

Suddenly it was April and Open House time. John had completed his staffing phase so had at least 16 to 18 friendly welcomers to the Sunday afternoon event. Family members helped conduct tours through the two-story building and the adjoining pilot plant. Each stop was manned by a staff member conversant with what work was done there. End point of the tour was the conference room for coffee, punch and trays of assorted home-made cookies and small frosted cakes.

Research Centers, of course, are Idea Centers and, at risk of missing a stand-out, few ideas are unlistened to. In the 1950s, the California Wine Institute had launched a campaign to take the "snobbery" out of wine-drinking, to educate consumers about wines and their place in the food and beverage picture. Many Americans were convinced that wine-drinking was a prerogative of the wealthy, that there were two kinds of wine, white and red, or that by stirring a cup of wine into a dish you were preparing would automatically make it super-special, thereby inflating your credibility with zealous "gourmets."

A San Francisco colleague, Jessica McLachlin, was Consumer Services Director of the Institute and oversaw the preparation of several informative booklets classifying wines by type and offering pointers on selection, storage, and service of wine. The Institute ran several magazine ads encouraging readers to familiarize themselves with wine and to enjoy it. In each ad there was the offer of a half-dozen tulip-shaped wine glasses for the (1950's) price of $5.95!

In the 1950's, wine shops were rare, especially wine-gift shops. Such shops, in addition to offering a stock of wines, would include all the accessory items relating to its service, from corkscrews and coasters, to plates, glasses and cheese boards. Why not, indeed, make them wine and cheese shops! Jessica approved the idea with enthusiasm. She knew of several wine-gift shops in California and they were very successful. When I discussed the idea with John, he considered it well worth developing and to talk it over with Cliff and Charlie for economic and marketing research input.

A temporary vacant office next to mine became the setting for our proposed shop, "The Wine Press." With the help of our kitchen manager, Jane Carlson, I became the collector of wine and cheese related items to display and to help the shop come to life. We declared the shop off-limits to curious staff members till opening day.

John had asked two top Peavey executives from the downtown offices to come to the presentation, since they would have a say in its approval. He prefaced his remarks by explaining that there were a number of directions that could be taken in further development. Cliff Fuller and Charlie Sutton, respectively, provided relevant economic and market research data. I reported my observations as a former food editor on recently changing wine consumption figures, both as a beverage and in culinary use.

Discussion was lively and reaction to "The Wine Press," rewarding. But objectivity prevailed: we were ahead of our time. The concept was valid and, we felt sure, would emerge—successfully,—in the future.

A basic element in the company's plan to enter the consumer market was the acquisition of successful established firms which were compatible with the Peavey reputation for fair business practices and good employee relations. Among them was Brownberry Ovens, founded by Catharine Clark as a small bakery in Oconomowoc, Wisconsin, and developed into a national success. She started with loaves of wonderful and worthy 100% whole wheat to a growing line of breads using other nutritious grains as well. All with satisfying texture, not "cottony," and very flavorful.

Northwest Fabrics was also acquired. Their stores supplied patterns, fabrics, threads, zippers and the many other items shopped for by women who love home sewing. And to those who consider it a money-saving measure.

My plan to drive to Dubuque for the long Easter week-end was advanced a day when Helen called on Wednesday. She was in our family home with Mom and Dad. Mom had taken a turn for the worse. Could I come earlier? Bill was on his way from Reno and Mary, from Connecticut. Mother had had a series of small strokes but a strong heartbeat, Dr. Gilloon explained. In these recent days she would often say, "I don't know why the Lord doesn't take me. I'm ready to go...." Never, ever was it her intent to question her dear Lord's wisdom!

She died peacefully, early in the afternoon on Good Friday. The "wake," or visitation, on Sunday and the funeral Mass on Easter Monday, in the Cathedral, where Mother had been baptized and had worshiped all her eighty-nine years. Easter lilies, scarlet and golden tulips, and baskets of wild flowers which she loved made the sanctuary look like the anteroom to Heaven.

I remained in Dubuque for the rest of the week. All of us wanted to put off our farewells to Dad. After sharing a beautiful life with his "Mamie" for almost seven decades, how he will miss her! But he was strong, faced reality, and always grateful for all God had given him and our family.

1973-1978

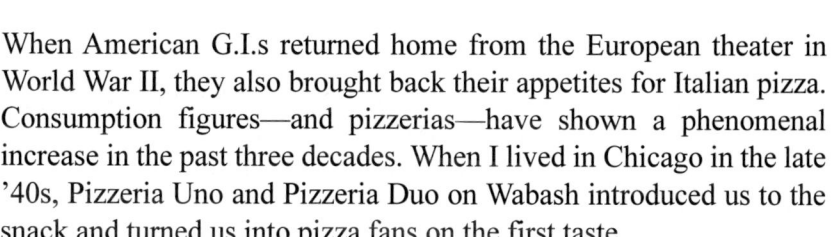

When American G.I.s returned home from the European theater in World War II, they also brought back their appetites for Italian pizza. Consumption figures—and pizzerias—have shown a phenomenal increase in the past three decades. When I lived in Chicago in the late '40s, Pizzeria Uno and Pizzeria Duo on Wabash introduced us to the snack and turned us into pizza fans on the first taste.

Our Research Center had a busy first four years and an interesting variety of projects to work on. The Research Center's candidate in the pizza race, after much testing and tasting, was a frozen rectangular pizza slice, to be heated in an electric toaster. Test-marketing rated it a winner of an idea. However, when distributed in wider market areas, a problem arose. If the pizza slice was toasted in certain makes of toasters on the market, the hot, flavorful topping would slip off to the bottom of the slot. Not the result a starved pizza fan was awaiting! Nor was it one facing the one charged with cleaning the toaster. For us, the immediate and over-riding concern was the safety issue. So, back to the Development Lab for a re-formulation solution.

Another project, the development of a group of salad/soup croutons, which would add interest and taste appeal to these popular menu choices. Following that project closely, was the development for the frozen food market of a line of favorite Italian entrees, reduced in calories but <u>not</u> in taste.

We certainly were not ignoring the basic products the Peavey name was known for, especially the whole-grain flours to go into whole-wheat bread, Swedish Limpa, Pumpernickel and other rye breads. Consumers were becoming more nutrition-conscious and we were eager to supply sound, understandable information to them.

For two years I'd been volunteering with the State Department of the Blind, writing and taping a weekly half-hour program on family health, "An Apple a Day." The program was broadcast over a private network to persons visually impaired. Their special radios were supplied by the State.

So many changes in the food field had been taking place during the sixties and seventies, and the Peavey Research Center was not immune to them. Science and technology were impacting almost every field. Our lives were captivated by—and being held captive to—the magic of electronics. The energy crisis was a very real concern. After analysis of the favorable record of the work of the Research Center during its first year, and projecting into the future, a significant decision was reached. In the early seventies, the "International Venture Research, a division of the Peavey Company," was announced as an outgrowth of the Chaska operation. "IVR" shifted to a heavy emphasis on science and technology, and the identification of new business opportunities.

I'd been making frequent trips to Dubuque. My father, now in his nineties, was coping well with his loneliness, not nearly as well with the severe arthritis that had hit him shortly before Mom's death. At that time we had arranged with a kind, reliable neighbor, Amanda Rowell, to be an "on-call" care-giver to Dad: she never failed to answer. Helen and John and various family members stopped by often at "383" to spend time with him. Almost every Saturday evening Dad would prepare a fried chicken feast for Helen and Gene's Farley family. Since the early sixties, two of his nieces were members of that family, brought there from Ireland by the generous hearts of their Aunt Helen and Uncle Gene. Pat, 17, and Phyllis, 13, were absorbed into our entire Holmberg clan with genuine warmth.

John stopped for coffee daily and did Dad's food shopping, equipped with a very detailed list. His son Michael, who worked close by, came regularly to eat lunch with Grandpa. Cousin Catharine was a frequent "carry-in" lunch partner, stopping on the way home from her half-day job to pick up a special treat. Afterward, a rousing session of dominoes.

The distance between Dubuque and Edina, a bit under 300 miles, gave me ideal time to analyze things. Dad had been on the giving side all the years I'd known and loved him. I didn't worry that he would not continue to receive that love and good care. But if I could help brighten his days and long evenings, even a little, I wanted so much to do that. On Monday, I told John Nelson of my decision to resign from Peavey, lined up a mover who would pack my furnishings, move them to Dubuque and into storage until notified. Within a week or two, I was driving to Dubuque, too. Moving into the century-plus home in the northeast hill country of Iowa.

In towns the size of Dubuque, the news grapevines have always functioned with remarkable speed. As my desk and heavy electronic typewriter, my files and bookcase were changing the landscape in one corner of our large kitchen, I was pleased to have phone calls welcoming me home. Particularly when several of these calls included either queries about my availability or an actual writing assignment. Barbara Shick's call was a pleasant surprise, a blend of the "availability" question and an invitation to lunch after I'd had time to get settled and her classes at Clarke College were over for the year. In 1970, Barbara had succeeded Sister Mary St. Clara. Sister had headed the Food and Nutrition Department for over 50 years and her record in placing dietetics majors in internship programs which led to very desirable positions following, was widely recognized. Barbara's M.S. degree in Chemistry equipped her well for the many changes and advances in the Food and Nutrition field. I looked forward to meeting her and I agreed to teach an Organization and Management Course for the 1975-76 academic year.

The next call was from Zelma Clark, art director at our local newspaper, the Telegraph Herald. An accomplished artist herself, she had become a one-woman crusader to add some zip to the current T-H ads. Could I provide her with some creative ideas for several accounts, with supporting copy? The quarter page ads were fun to do, converted from concept and copy into creative etchings by Zelma. Three accounts were an interesting mix: a supermarket, an optical shop and a sportswear store. Dad found all this activity an exciting change from the loneliness and monotony of his previous schedule. A nap after dinner was still his routine. Then, with a degree of wonder, he'd settle into his rocking chair to watch color TV. When I'd take him a cup of coffee with a couple of home-baked cookies, his day was made. "You make me feel like royalty!"

Soon after Zelma's call the T-H food editor rang me. By that time Spring was making an auspicious entrance, which we developed into a full-page story on the vegetable garden's bounty. Scheduled just in time for the opening of Dubuque's fabulous Farmers' Market on Saturday, May 24, 1975. Dubuque's location in the tri-states area of Iowa, Wisconsin and Illinois, with fertile land and the area's large segment of skilled, hard-working farmers was reflected in the blue-ribbon quality of the produce, the variety of offerings and their appealing displays, evidence of what a gift we have in our country's food supply.

Several weeks later the TH contacted me again. They were planning a special section in a late October Sunday issue—"The Best of 20 Recipe Roundups." The Recipe Roundup was an annual "event" in Dubuque. A contest in which TH readers would enter favorite recipes in defined categories and then wait with baited breath, hoping to win a "Best." There would be 2nd and 3rd places, too, but "Best" was "Best."

My challenge would be the selection of 100 Best Award-winning recipes which appeared in Roundups from the first-ever one in 1956 to 1976, the planned special issue. Two "decades" worth! Many of the paper's readers, I was told, had saved every annual issue. They'd really appreciate this 1976 topper-offer, I felt. So I accepted the challenge and began my sleuthing.

I had hardly started the Roundup project when a cold my father had contacted turned into pneumonia and Dr. Gilloon insisted, as gently as possible, on his hospitalization. A hospitalization that extended almost a month. Most of those anxious days and nights were marked by his calm, and his reassurance to us that he was not afraid to die, that he had had a wonderful life and "was ready to go." (Not an overtly pious man, our 92-year old father was one of the most sincerely Christian persons I had ever known.) How we wished that Father Loras might be there to celebrate Dad's funeral Mass in the Cathedral. But clearly Dad was confident that all of his dear departed ones would be waiting in eternity to welcome him. Loras and Mother, of course, her two little miscarried souls and the twins who died within an hour of birth, present so briefly to be loved and cared for.

Farm Journal had been one of the leading farm magazines in publishing for an amazing length of time. Founded in 1877 by a Quaker, farmer and journalist, Wilmer Atkinson. The fledgling magazine's mission was to serve the farmers in the rich, productive land of the states neighboring Pennsylvania. Headquarters of the magazine was Philadelphia. Emphasis was on providing common-sense information to farmers and their wives. My contact with "Farm Journal," of course, was in the food area, in food and nutrition coverage in their monthly issues, and in a long list of cookbooks, both soft-cover and hard-cover. All of them with recipes which, I'm sure, would make Wilmer Atkinson proud that his "common sense" approach to providing information has endured. The books have contributed a great deal to the well-deserved reputation farm wives have for being culinary experts.

I was pleased then, when "Farm Journal" asked if I'd be interested in collaborating with them on a cookbook dealing with the energy crisis and ways to help ease it. The idea of recruiting the oven to help achieve that goal was not new, especially to savvy farm wives. But oven meals, carefully planned in advance, can conserve energy and precious time, and provide satisfying, nutritious meals as well. Simon and Schuster published *Great Dishes From the Oven* in 1977. Not a big book, no breath-taking photos, but a hard-cover treasury of recipes bound to become family favorites. And save energy and money as well!

1978-1983

The 1978 fall semester at Clarke and my commitment to teach the Organization and Management class in the Food and Nutrition Department (at 8 a.m.!) three days a week, came quickly. At about the same time, a Cedar Rapids advertising agency, Fultz, LaCasse, was opening a branch office in Dubuque. They had just moved into a downtown office and the staff would come the following week. I called the office to inquire whether the agency had any food accounts and might be in need of anyone with my background and experience. The manager, Robert E. Buckley (Bob), was holding the fort and answered my phone call. He gave me a positive answer to both parts of my question. Could I come in for an interview the next day? I could and did.

The agency's major account was Swiss Valley Farms, an association of area dairy farmers who marketed quality milks and cheeses. My initial assignment was the writing and taping of a series of radio scripts. Commercials to familiarize listeners with the Swiss Valley presence in our area markets. A short time later we produced several TV commercials featuring a young family, enthusiastic consumers of SV products. Bob and his wife, Lois, had two young sons who were the picture of health and vitality and a personable friend, Helen Kramer, whom we cast as a model homemaker and the boys' mother. Bob was great to work with, always ready to entertain new ideas, yet also sure of his goals. He was creative, with gentle Irish wit, pleased, I believe, that my Swedish name "Holmberg" concealed Sullivan, Cavanaugh, Grandfield and assorted other Irish connections.

At this time, many major food companies supplied excellent educational materials to Home Economics teachers. Many advertised in one or both highly respected Home Economics magazines, "Forecast" and "What's New in Home Economics." Among these companies was Ralston Purina, a St. Louis cereal company. In a late-summer phone call, they asked if I could develop several double-page spreads featuring their cereals. Perhaps as ingredients for quick-to-prepare, tasty main dishes, or in combination with other nutritious ingredients, for snack-time. In the late forties, their Home Economics kitchen had come up with an idea for such a snack that took consumers by storm. Geared to simple home preparation, it combined several varieties of their Chex cereal with pretzel sticks, Spanish ("red-skin") peanuts, garlic powder and Worcestershire Sauce. The mixture was then stirred into a large shallow baking pan containing melted margarine or heated cooking oil and placed in a 300° F oven for long, slow roasting, stirring occasionally.

Known as "Nuts and Bolts," the mix showed up at innumerable holiday parties its first year—and "ever after." Prompted by its consumer acceptance, Ralston Purina was soon marketing a line of the packaged ready-to-eat CHEX snacks. Working with the Ralston advertising department on the project was great. Food and nutrition professionals were beginning to see increasing evidence of their on-going efforts at preaching the "eating right" gospel.

"INSTITUTIONS," a semi-monthly magazine for quantity food service professionals, gave me an opportunity to reach a huge nutrition-aware readership: hotels, restaurants, hospitals, schools, etc, when they accepted a two-part series of columns. The first was "Gearing Menus to Ride the Healthy Food Trend." The second, directed to health care facilities and school food service managers was "Nutrition in Neon." Considering the ever-increasing number of meals eaten outside the home, being armed with a sound knowledge and a consistent application of nutrition principles is a key to success in these fields.

On the heels of wrapping up the Ralston Purina project, I had had a phone call from a textbook publisher, Wadsworth Publishing, inquiring whether I would be interested in authoring a college text on meal management in our rapidly changing society. Socio-economic developments continue to bring about modified life-styles. The "three-meals-a-day" eating pattern has almost vanished. Convenience foods and innovative equipment have certainly simplified food preparation, but have not made the meal manager's job less important. Nutritious, satisfying meals don't just happen. Sound management techniques in shopping, food storage, safety and sanitation are essential. So too is the presentation and serving of the prepared food. The textbook project was too challenging to side-step!

Authoring the book, I realized, would be steady, absorbing work. After settling on an effective approach and planning a workable time-table, I stopped by Clarke and discussed the project with my friend, Barbara Schick. She graciously lined up some of the established and recently published Home Economics texts that I could see what the competition was offering. Later, in search for black and white plates to illustrate the section on Food Production and Distribution, I called "Design Photography," listed in our local phone directory. I talked with Ken Smith, photographer-owner. He was sure he'd have some prints to fill my needs, so I dropped by his studio the next day to pick them up. He had about a half-dozen set aside, most of them right on target, and was pleased that I could use them. He was interested in my background and in learning more about food photography. He had done some product shots for Fleur de Lis, a local meat packer for use in package illustrations, but was aiming for the opportunity to do their finished-food shots, then being done by a Chicago studio. I explained my time-consuming commitment to Wadsworth but urged him to keep in touch. He did that. And somewhat later did get the finished food job. He called to report his good news and to check on my availability to work with him on the project. We blocked out a time for planning and a tentative date for shooting the three photos. How could I *not* make time to help him!

The shoot went well and the client was pleased with the photos. They told Ken they'd like him to do more work for them. The company was undergoing a name change: from "Fleur de Lis" to "Dubuque Packing Company" or "Dupaco." Plans to introduce a new product line were underway. The client asked if I would have time to do the preliminary product testing required for the data used on each product package. (I found the time, a pleasant and fairly short change of pace from text-booking.)

Meal Management Today was published in 1980. What a happy surprise on a cold, snowy Saturday morning, to receive a carton of the complimentary author's copies! A happiness shared first with my family—<u>and</u> on Sunday, at beautiful snow blanketed Mount Carmel with my dear teacher and friend, Sister Mary St. Clara. Retiring after six decades of service at Clarke, she was for several years care-giver for her sister, Mary, also a retired teacher in an apartment close to the college. After Mary's death Sister moved to Marian Hall Infirmary at Mount Carmel, which was not far from my apartment. Her joy at perusing the textbook expanded my happiness liters and liters.

Adoptions of the text by colleges and universities well-known for their programs in dietetics, home economics, food science and food service management were gratifying to Wadsworth and, of course, to me. Suddenly, however, in this era of mergers and acquisitions, Wadsworth was purchased by a British publishing firm. They would be reshaping their list of offerings. Although I could understand that *Meal Management Today*, tailored to our country's readership, would be a logical casualty, I felt like Chicken Little bemoaning the news that "the sky is falling!"

Fortunately, word of the book's demise circulated at the annual national convention of the American Home Economic Association being held that week. One of the exhibitors, Waveland Press, a Chicago area firm apparently heard opportunity knocking. He phoned to inquire whether I had yet made plans to place the book with another publisher. Since I had not, we arranged to meet early the next week to discuss the mechanics of a transfer process, whether any changes in content might be called for, and financial terms. We also agreed that a lively new cover would distinguish the book from the original. The new book was published in 1983. The new cover, front and back, displayed shallow baskets holding assortments of bright-colored, nutritious foods from the basic food groups, against a cobalt-blue background. A cover conceived by a creative, imaginative artist.

1983-1988

Bolstered by enthusiastic response to the new *Meal Management Today* (and relieved that the sky was not falling,) I rewarded myself by plunging into a tempting stack of books I hadn't had time to read during the past two years. Our local library had begun a program of one-minute book reviews to follow the daily noon-time news. Several of us volunteers agreed to condense the content of a book into 60 seconds, and to tape-record it, an intriguing challenge! Also, a pleasant surprise, to hear from the mix of faithful listeners to the reviews. Teachers catching the reviews before hurrying on to their classes, homemakers in the middle of late lunch, and Mac, my gas station man. The project became almost addictive. In the five years the program had run, I'd done close to 90 reviews.

Happily, for both Design Photography and me, Dupaco was keeping us busy. The client's voiced appreciation of our work was always good to hear. So, too, was my watching Ken's gradual awareness of how he and his camera could draw out the beauty of food in a well-composed set-up. It prompted him to ask what I would think about inviting a few of his food client prospects to the studio for a real live demonstration of what goes into a food shoot. Our goal: to de-mystify the widely held myth that a big part of food photography is fakery (imitation fruits, vegetables and assorted other foods, shaving cream to substitute for whipped cream, on and on).

We planned a simple, attractive set, with an irresistible-looking cheesecake on a pedestal cake stand. Encircling the base of the cheesecake were glossy deep green lemon leaves holding clusters of cool green grapes. Dessert china, silverware and napkins, as well as a handsome coffee carafe alongside. Four duplicate cheesecakes "on call" in the refrigerator, one or two for likely replacements of the starring item's time under the lights. The others for our guests to enjoy "after the show." Interest was high and Ken felt we had made an impact. He also realized that, although gaining a couple more food accounts could be worthwhile, he would need to have more staff to handle increased workloads.

Working with Ken was rewarding. He had the sharp vision, the keen sense of design <u>and</u> the patience required of a good food photographer. He recognized how quickly a beautiful food set-up deteriorates under the camera by the time the critical step of lighting is accomplished. That chanting "abracadabra" over the wilted set-up <u>does</u> <u>not</u> rejuvenate it. An exact duplicate must replace it— without delay.

A photographer-friend of Ken's, Bob Coyle, had set up a studio recently on Dubuque's north side. A former award-winning Telegraph Herald staff member, he and I had met when he shot several photos of me to accompany the big October 1976 Anniversary feature, "The Best of Twenty Recipe Round-ups." Also, on publication of "Great Dishes From The Oven." He called to inquire whether I would be available to work with him on a project with Shullsburg Creamery, Shullsburg, Wisconsin. A brochure-type catalog of their offerings of top-quality cheeses and country-smoked meats. The Irish, German and Scandinavian immigrants who settled this area in the mid-1800s left a rich legacy in cheese-and sausage-making. Now, not quite two centuries later, we're still relishing the products of that legacy.

Bob's newspaper experience in photographing a diverse assortment of people, places and happenings made him wonderfully perceptive. The Shullsburg catalog photos were only 4" by 3 ½" inches, but were close-up shots. He had caught the velvety smoothness of the cheeses, the wine-red richness of the sausages and the interesting texture of the whole-grain breads. My artist friend, Zelma Clark, enjoyed assisting me in composing the photos. She, Bob and I were a pleased pictorial trio when we reviewed the developed shots early the next week.

Soon Bob and I worked on another project, one that was also basically, a listing of gift offerings by a cheese company in northern Illinois. Instead of being in booklet form though, it was a folder-type, resembling a large square road map. There would be no finished-food shots in the folder, the client had decided, but it would contain a number of standard product displays, from small to large to too large.

The cheese plant, where the photography would be done, was about 40 miles from Dubuque. We estimated that it would be a three-day job. Bob picked me up for the drive there the first two days. I would drive the third, so if I had to leave early to keep a late-afternoon doctor's appointment in Dubuque, I could. On that second day we'd had misgivings when the client insisted that every single item they marketed be included in a veritable "cheese mountain" rivaling the height if not the magnificence of Mt. McKinley.

We had not quite completed the job and I was confident that Bob could wrap it up. He'd agreed to shoot a photo of the husband-wife owners, which they'd requested on the spur of the moment just before I left.

The third day had been fairly sunny on my early morning drive over but around noon, the sun was intimidated by heavy steel-gray clouds. When we broke for cheese sandwiches a dense fog was taking over. The slow, scary drive on curvy—and almost invisible Highway 20—had lengthened to 400 miles, by the time I turned up my drive and reached (limply) for my garage door-opener.

The latter years of this time span were marked with joy-packed family occasions. First in mid-May of 1987 was Chris's ordination to the Roman Catholic priesthood in Bridgeport's St. Augustine's Cathedral. A touching, heart-warming liturgy! Dinner at the Gaelic-American Club after, with distinctive Irish music playing softly in the background. The next day, the new Father Christopher J. Walsh offered his First Mass in the family's home church in Fairfield, Our Lady of the Assumption. He used the same gold chalice which his Uncle Loras had used almost three decades before. At dinner following Mass, family and close friends reflected Chris's radiant joy and gratitude.

A few months later, Father Chris performed the wedding ceremony for his youngest sister, Ann, and Michael Henderson. As a grad school student at the University of Colorado at Boulder and since then, working in a lab there, she was active in the Newman Club, an organization for Catholic students. Their wedding had been scheduled for the chapel there. However, only a few months before the ceremony, a fire intervened and completely destroyed the chapel. A frenzied "church search" led to an incredibly pleasing outcome. An old abbey a short distance from Boulder with a small rustic church beside it. The widely circulated report: that this site was where "Lilies of the Field" starring Sidney Poitier was filmed—and where they still bloom on TV every now and then!

As summer of 1988 neared, a Walsh family friend mentioned to Father Chris and Mary Elizabeth that they'd like to invite Mary and Noel to stay in their Berkshire home for a week while they were traveling. Noel, Mary's husband, had office commitments he couldn't change. But the siblings and friends would be welcome on a "short-stay basis", as space allowed. Part of their thoughtful plan included me in their invitation. I'd never been in much of western Massachusetts and the Berkshire Mountains were new to me. Father Chris drove his Mom and me up from Bridgeport to a lightly-wooded area: tall, deep green evergreens which seemed to be stretching to reach the cloudless blue sky. The home was large and welcoming, as big-hearted as our generous hosts.

Michael Walsh and wife Julie were our first Berkshire guests, driving from Hartford for a 2-day stay. Typically, they came bearing gifts, a specialty of his, Seafood Lasagna, with ingredients for a tossed salad, pre-buttered French bread, foil wrapped and ready for the oven. A skilled lawyer, Michael had become interested in culinary skills and had asked if he could do supper. So, after juice, coffee and scones on their mid-morning arrival, we decided to tour the Norman Rockwell studio near-by. A serene pastoral setting which must have contributed to his generation of cartoons depicting daily living in calm and in war-torn days. Rockwell's talent for gentle humor, touching all generations, earned him regular appearances on the popular Saturday Evening Post magazine.

We returned to the house in late afternoon. As dusk was approaching Father Chris offered Mass on the deck outside the spacious living-dining room. Chef Michael managed the Lasagna Supper, (accepting some assistance from Mary and me). Julie poured the wine. Being together was such a blessing and before we were aware, 10:30 and bedtime broke in. I had recalled that Better Homes and Gardens had covered one of the remaining Shaker Villages in 1964 at the time I joined the staff. Shortly, a restored Hancock Village Museum had become a very popular tourist attraction. Our itinerary for tomorrow!

The day at Hancock catapulted us back in time. An off-shoot of the Quaker faith, Shakers lived a simple, prayerful life, firmly believing in hard work but also in celibacy. In close touch with the land and family, they developed the mail-order seed business. Shaker-designed furniture and Shaker architecture became recognized for its beauty and simplicity.

The second Walsh daughter, Kathy, her husband Jim Alber and their four delightful "little women" spent a day with us. All of the girls, under 12, we explored the area, by car <u>and</u> by foot, pretending we were seasoned mountain climbers. (Aileen, the youngest, was carried in her Daddy's back-pack.) Early dinner at a friendly family inn before the weary mountaineers headed home to Connecticut.

1988-1993

Back in the fifties, many graduate home economists employed by food companies and equipment manufacturers were responsible for planning and conducting programs promoting the merits of the company's products. Program requests came year-round from all over the United States. They were from various women's and men's clubs and, occasionally, from young adult and scouting groups eager to explore culinary activity as a hobby. Programmers had large, heavy suitcases of kitchen gear, serving pieces and attractive props to wrestle with, particularly if traveling by train, to keep a program commitment. They sometimes characterized themselves as being "one-fifth Madam Curie, one-fifth home economist, one-fifth Joan Crawford and two-fifths pack-horse." (Clearly, as the years went on, that definition called for cinematic up-dating!)

At Armour programs, those attending were invited to sign up for a monthly "Kitchen Service Bulletin," pre-punched for insertion into a 3-ring binder. The Bulletin contained newly-developed recipes with black and white photos as well as timely "neighbor to neighbor" product information, which included "how-to" steps in recipes when they would be helpful. If you were already on the mailing list and the mother of small children, you were especially appreciative of a cartoon strip on the bottom of the end page of the 4-page Bulletin. It depicted the day-by-day activities and antics of a happy, energetic family of pudgy, personable porkers. Youngsters were fascinated by the cartoon and eagerly awaited delivery of the Bulletin every month.

The Bulletin had been one of my initial responsibilities after joining Armour in 1951, and a responsibility I savored. A few of the numerous topics we covered over the years were:

- Old-fashioned Stews
- The First (Breeze-easy) Thanksgiving Dinner
- Blue-Sky Cooking
- Speaking of Sandwiches
- Party-going Cakes
- Play Up That Breakfast Protein

Around that time, the emergence of TV food shows was limiting guest appearances of these home economists. The shows began to feature "hosts" many of whom displayed minimal knowledge of food or food preparation and, often, focused entirely on appetite satisfaction. But TV show producers learned that viewers wanted sound, basic information about food, clear instructions in preparation methods and appealing, nutritious recipes. Recipes that didn't require a trip to the supermarket for a half-dozen ingredients (which you may use only once), even before you donned your apron. Viewers were looking for guidance in food purchasing and storage as well as in meal-planning. The host of a successful food show had to be qualified. Being a handsome or pretty "foodist" wasn't enough.

As the popularity of TV food shows increased, changes in magazine food articles were also occurring. Whether the changes reflected a new casual approach to eating or a friendly competition among art directors and food photographers was pure conjecture. An informative, well-written story on sandwiches and sandwich-making, for example, covering all types—plain every day, open-face, club, grilled, dips, party cut-outs, etc. might be illustrated by a skyscraper structure of two or three meats, assorted cheeses, tomatoes, onions, cucumbers, lettuce and "drizzle-downs" of creamy salad dressing. Colorful and striking! But more approachable with a low-level explosive, a stack of paper napkins and a bib than with a knife and fork. Beautiful roasted meats and poultry were being over-adorned with unfamiliar garnishes which often over-lapped the platter's edge. In casseroles which, the article promised, would become your family's favorites, the ingredients were often unrecognizable. More attention was paid to the "fol-de-rol" than to the food itself.

As I'd been witnessing the many changes in the food field and in the eating patterns and ways in which food was being prepared, an idea for a magazine article popped into my head. Friends were surprised that with a few exceptions, I was clinging to "from scratch" food preparation, particularly in baking. They considered me a magic wand-waver as they enjoyed apricot-bran muffins or cranberry cream scones fresh from the oven, 100% whole wheat bread or Lemon Daisy or Chocolate-Mocha birthday cake. Yet I did applaud the mix-makers for the incredible improvement they had made in the quality of most mixes since they were first introduced. <u>And</u> in their creativity in development of new mixes.

I queried Jeanne Voltz, food editor at Woman's Day Magazine, a very competent one. We viewed food writing through similar lenses. In my query about the home-made mix idea, I detailed the direction I planned to go and described a number of "suggested additions" that I had in mind. Jeanne's response was prompt and positive. The article, "Fix-This-Mix Short Order-Casseroles," would appear in the September 13, 1988 issue of Woman's Day.

The handy-to-have-on-hand mix was based on a combination of:

2 c medium egg noodles

<u>OR</u>

¾ c long-grain white rice

2 tsp <u>each</u> instant beef <u>or</u> chicken flavor bouillon, and parsley flakes

1 tsp instant minced onion

1/8 tsp pepper

To use: Measure mix ingredients into a 1 ½ qt casserole or shallow baking dish. Dot with 1 tsp butter or margarine. If preparing noodle mix, stir in 1 ½ cups boiling water. (If preparing <u>rice</u> mix, 1 ¾ c boiling water.) Stir until well blended. Cover tight with foil. Bake in preheated 350° F oven until liquid is absorbed (and noodles are firm), 20 to 25 minutes. Remove casserole from oven and with a rubber spatula gently stir in the set-aside "suggested additions." Return casserole uncovered to oven and continue baking as directed in recipe, or until thoroughly heated. Makes 4 servings.

In two of the seven or eight casseroles featured in the Woman's Day article, one made with noodles and chicken-flavor bouillon, the other with long-grain rice and chicken or beef bouillon, were photographed and photogenic. The additions used were:

Curried Chicken and Mushrooms

1 cup sour cream

1 small can mushrooms, drained (reserving ¼ cup liquid)

2 teaspoons curry powder

1 ½ cups cubed cooked chicken

2 Tablespoons chopped pimento

Raisins and shredded coconut (optional)

Prepare chicken-flavor noodle mix. Stir together sour cream, reserved mushroom liquid and curry powder; pour over hot noodles. Gently stir in chicken, mushrooms and pimento. Return casserole to oven and bake for 25 minutes or until thoroughly heated. If desired, top with raisins and coconut. Makes 4 servings.

Green and Gold Rice Bake

½ cup minced parsley

2 Tablespoons snipped chives

1 cup shredded Cheddar cheese

1 egg, slightly beaten

¾ cup milk

Parmesan cheese

Prepare beef-flavor rice mix, using 1 ¾ cups boiling water. Stir parsley, chives and shredded cheese into hot rice. Stir together egg and milk; pour over rice mixture. Return casserole to oven and bake 25 to 30 minutes until firm. Sprinkle with Parmesan cheese. Makes 4 servings.

Several weeks later, I was meeting Zelma Clark for lunch at a new downtown restaurant. "The New French Café" was being operated by a French chef said to be long on experience and skill. As we perused the handsome tall maroon menus, I mentioned a food column I'd written when living in Chicago years ago. Giving it a light, humorous twist, it was a capsule guide to French menu terms, since those terms are borrowed for menus internationally. The column was published in the June 2, 1963 edition of the Sunday Chicago Tribune. I'd thought about a re-write but hadn't ever gotten around to it. However, Zelma and I really enjoyed our luncheon and made so many trips back to the restaurant that I promised Zelma I'd do that rewrite. The Telegraph Herald published the re-write with a striking color photo, on the front page of the Sunday Food Section, July 1, 1998.

1993-1998

The late nineties . . . and the world was caught up in discussing the approaching millennium. Granted, the end of the nineties—<u>and</u> the close of the twentieth century—were not too far distant. However, to suspect that some dire, dramatic event might happen (like the end of the world) wasn't very palatable either. Such predictions had been voiced previously but, happily, had not occurred.

In the early nineties I had begun volunteering at the BVM Infirmary, Marian Hall, at the southeast end of Grandview, not far from my home. At that time, our Public Library was distributing books every month to over a dozen health-care facilities. They would remove and replace one-third of "old" books with new titles. Fiction, non-fiction, history, biography, mystery, spiritual reading. On one morning a week, a little before 10 o'clock, I'd report to the Activity Room where Marge Beutin was Activities Director. She'd post me on patients' conditions, and discharges or admissions, and general news, and, with my loaded book cart, I'd head for the floors.

Almost all the Marian Hall residents were intelligent, avid readers. Most had teaching backgrounds, in small towns and in large cities and at various educational levels: elementary, secondary, college. A number of them had taught in graduate school as well as in centers in Alaska, Ecuador and Hawaii. Visiting with them was one flashback after another. They had been such a significant part of my life. With many of them I shared a bulging bank of memories. I anticipated my weekly Book Cart activity as a real joy, not a task. The atmosphere of warmth and genuine caring which prevailed at Marian Hall encouraged my routine of early arrival. My departure too, almost always ran into overtime.

As I'd walk down the long first floor hallway and out into the crisp wintry air, sincere expressions of gratitude came from everyone, from cleaning ladies and kitchen aides to nurses and the administrator. I was touched. And then I thought, "I should be thanking them!" Not one of the sisters I'd visited or any of the Marian Hall staff had ever mentioned the millennium. Had I brought the subject up, I am 100% confident what the response would be. Maybe not an exact quote of the prayer of St. Thomas More, but certainly, the embodiment of a Christian's faith. "Never trouble thy mind about what shall happen in this world. Nothing can come but what God wills."

Very soon, Sister Mary Faith Lautz was assigned as Director of the Roberta Kuhn Center and, as each predecessor had done, she gave it a new, fresh dimension. An accomplished artist, she had taught art—and much more—and had also been an administrator in elementary and secondary schools in Phoenix, Wichita, Kansas City, MO, Milwaukee, San Jose and Fairbanks, Alaska. She served in pastoral ministry in Anchorage and in Holy Cross, Alaska. She was particularly challenged by work "out in the bush country." Her art classes at the Roberta Kuhn Barn attracted students with varying degrees of talent. I had registered for a once-a-week class in Drawing and was captivated by her class. Sister Faith's expertise in gently guiding even those on the lower end of the talent scale was remarkable. I recall her pausing at my table one day to assist me with a problem on a project. As she was applying her know-how, my reaction was, "She's only making it worse!" Then, as if by magic, my hoped-for masterpiece was on its way. The difference between talent and trying!

Although I'd succeeded in keeping my mother's Christmas cactus thriving (with the faithful support of my Dubuque nephew, "Cactus Man" Michael Holmberg), I'd never had the chance to do much gardening. But Sister Faith and I shared a love of reading, so when she asked if I'd consider starting a Roberta Kuhn Reading Group, I couldn't refuse. Because space in the Barn was limited, our first "group" of three met in the Mount Carmel library. Two dear BVM friends, Sister Mary Jocile Valliere and Sister Mary Gregory Mackin, as a show of their support, I'm sure, and the third, a rather shy laywoman from an outlying rural area. From that unspectacular beginning however, 18 years later we had 26 members in our Reading for Enjoyment group.

The thrust of the group, as the name suggests, was to be a pleasant conversational gathering. We would select from the broad range of worthwhile books of all types, but there would be no homework or written reports, no tests. An important factor in this approach was that each of the Fall and Spring semesters was actually only 12 to 14 weeks in length. In our beloved Midwest, early winter onsets, late spring arrivals, heavy snowfalls and torrential rains which cause flooding rob class schedules of meeting days. As the group increased we were blessed with a wide diversity in vocational and educational backgrounds, in nationalities, in income levels and travel experience. That diversity enriched discussion rather than limiting it. So many contrasting viewpoints were revealed.

Some of our favorites in that 18-year span:

Simon's Night—Jon Hassler

Dakota—Kathleen Norris

Truman—David McCullough

Body and Soul—Frank Conroy

Stones for Ibarra—Harriet Doerr

The Color of Water—James McBride

An American Childhood—Annie Dillard

Girl with the Pearl Earring—Tracy Chevalier

Wedding Dress—Virginia Ellis

Marie Antoinette—Antonia Fraser

The Secret Life of Bees—Sue Monk Kidd

Bobos in Paradise—David Brooks

The Kite Runner—Khaled Hosseini

Madonnas of Leningrad—Debra Dean

Devil in the White City—Erik Larson

Dear James—Jon Hassler
(Made into the movie, "A Green Journey," starring Angela Lansbury.)

At the same time that Sister Faith had returned to Mount Carmel, another highly-qualified BVM arrived. Sister Margaret Houlihan had taught in Ecuador for almost a decade. Then she was brought to Chicago to teach Spanish to priests of the archdiocese as parishes were welcoming large numbers of Spanish immigrants. Very quickly she was teaching Spanish at Roberta Kuhn Center, a beginning class and a Continuing Spanish class. I'd told Sister Margaret how much I wanted to register for the Beginners' group but that my Reading Group was conflicting. Her response, "Oh, my dear, come to the Continuing Class. You'll catch up!" I'd have preferred not to question this wise woman's counsel, but I explained what few Spanish words and phrases were in my lexicon. But she insisted.

At the very first session of Continuing Spanish, Sister ran audiotapes of Spanish songs and dramatic readings. The group joined in song, quite beautifully. (I simply "audited!") The device, I would learn later, was to teach us the rhythm and pacing of the language. I remained in the class for both semesters that year. Only occasionally would we follow the audio-tape format, and I did try to work in some study on the side. (I doubt if I will ever be selected as an Ambassadress to a Spanish-speaking country.)

In early May, to mark the end of the Center's year, an annual tea and exhibit of the students' work has been held in the Barn. What an impressive display of accomplishments, made possible by the many volunteer instructors who contribute their time and talent so generously to hundreds of appreciative seniors! There are hundreds of appreciative viewers, for partakers of another impressive display: a second table of assorted finger foods, appetizers, open-face sandwiches, cheeses, salted nuts, candies, small cakes and a dream-like assortment of cookies, cookies, cookies! Side tables hold fresh-brewed coffee and iced fruit punch, to help convert the Barn into a charming popular café.

1998-2003

Reaching 80 a decade ago hadn't seemed like a big milestone. I continued teaching part-time, handling a few occasional writing assignments and enjoying the volunteering. Rarely would I skip my daily 3 ½ mile walk around the Mt. Carmel grounds overlooking the Mississippi. A river that I'm afraid we took for granted. Often busy with barge traffic, sometimes iced over in winter, but in summer, alive with recreational boating and commercial steamboat travel. My usual wayfarer was my neighbor, Mary Wiederholt, faithful-care giver to her husband Floyd as he fought advanced Parkinson's disease with incredible courage. Mary was ever-available, too, to take over smoothing things out for her younger daughter, Helen, and her young children, Katie and Michael. Her other daughter, Ann, was enthusiastic about her new job in a wine and gift shop recently opened on renovated lower Main.

The year I returned to Dubuque, 1975, two men who definitely had been "thinking outside the box" started the Elderhostel program. Marty Knowlton, a social activist, and David Bianco, a university administrator, were friends and conceived the idea of "lifetime learning." A wide diversity of post-high school level courses, with highly qualified instructors, would be offered to elders at attractive travel destinations. <u>And</u>, importantly, at reasonable cost. In its infancy, Elderhostel programs were located mainly in domestic sites. Now, they've flourished for over three decades, and the world seems to be their stage.

At our coffee break after my frosty 8 a.m. classes at Clarke these days, Barbara Schick and I often talk Elderhostel. We both have friends who've attended some of the programs and have given them enthusiastic reports. We've checked their summer offerings and settled on a program at Lakeside College near Sheboygan, Wisconsin. Leaving Dubuque on a hot, sticky afternoon in July, we were looking forward to cooler, less humid climes. We arrived at the college dorms in time to sign in and unpack. A cordial welcome and brief orientation dinner helped to acquaint us with the two dozen or so other hostelers. After the group's introductions and a little about work background and any programs previously attended, Barb and I were impressed with the interesting mix of members.

At that time enrollment was for three of the courses offered. Two of them would be held in the morning and the third, after noon dinner. Except for Monday, the first days of classes, the balance of each day constituted free time for hostelers, a chance to explore their surroundings.

On the first Monday, following the third class, a bus was waiting to take us to a U.S. Coast Guard Station in Sheboygan for a submarine tour. Clearly our group of two dozen had to be sub-divided into sixes, which itself made sardine-pack! But after our viewing of the interior and hearing simplified explanations of equipment and fittings, we regrouped in the Station's meeting room. The officer in charge gave a very understandable overview of the submarine's functions and fielded questions on the Coast Guard's duties as we enjoyed soft drinks and chips.

Neighboring the Coast Guard Station was the intriguing village of Kohler, developed from a plain, every-day plumbing fixtures company to a highly successful designer of high-fashion bathrooms, saunas, and whirlpools. Our tour of the Kohler showroom was especially eye-opening to those elderhostelers who might even recall heating water for their Saturday night baths.

Another one of our three courses was a development story, too. It documented the success of a group of magazines of special interest to rural women proficient in meal preparation and keenly aware of the importance of "eating right." Our class was invited to visit their test kitchens in nearby Greendale and hear their story. As well, of course, as to sample some of the simplest but most truly gourmet dishes ever.

For Barb and me, satisfaction with our initial Elderhostel program was total. When Phil Swift, a Platteville friend, called one evening the following Spring and asked whether I'd be interested in signing up for an Elderhostel in August at the University of Wisconsin—Platteville branch. A university friend of his was registering students and Phil mentioned me to him as a possible prospect. "You'd be in an interesting atmosphere," Phil added, "the Chicago Bears will be there in training camp!" Fail-proof evidence when I did attend: the presence in their parking lot of so many glitzy, power-packed Harley-Davidsons.

For a number of years, Platteville's Shakespeare Theater, co-directed by two University professors, had been one of the area's leading summer attractions. I chose their class on the history of the theater as my third course. The wife of one director was costume mistress. She explained to the class the challenges presented in dressing the thespians. Particularly the super-active duelists and other combatants in their tight-fitting breeches and jackets. The solution was carefully sewn on hooks and eyes instead of stitches, zippers or Velcro. The search for fabrics which "looked Shakespearian" took time, too. The search, to her surprise, often ended at Wal-Mart.

2003-2008

I've begun to realize that life does give you signals as the aging process is underway. Even after my diagnosis of macular degeneration, changes seemed minimal. I squinted, of course, checked on my prescription for eye glasses, and welcomed my neighbor's willingness to thread sewing machine needles for me. An incident one gray overcast morning on my way to Mass sounded a clear, undeniable signal. I had slowed for the Locust—Highway 20 intersection, reputed to be one of the area's most dangerous, so was prepared for a sudden light change—to red. The object very close ahead of me, although resembling a dandelion gone to seed, was indeed the derriere of a pick-up truck! The encounter reinforced my wavering decision to give up driving. I sold my Lumina in 2007.

Barb Schick and I had registered for an Elderhostel at the University of Minnesota shortly after our first hostel (while I was still driving). Because university dormitories, where we ordinarily would be housed, were being renovated, we were assigned to a hotel on Nicollet Mall, a favorite shopping haunt of mine. One of our classes was "Five Great Minnesota Authors" conducted by a Yale Professor Emeritus. The five authors and perhaps their most noteworthy works:

- Sinclair Lewis—*Main Street*
- F. Scott Fitzgerald—*The Great Gatsby*
- Ole Rolvaag—*Giants in the Earth*
- Jon Hassler—*Staggerford, Simon's Night, and A Green Journey*
- Bill Holm—*Boxelder Bug Variations*

Our instructor was a wellspring of information about each of these authors. He pointed out the enduring impact *Main Street* has had on sanitation and safety in the food industry. F. Scott Fitzgerald and his Zelda may be most remembered as icons of the jazz age. My St. Paul friends, from Army days, Tan and Norm McVeigh, lived in a charming (although 4th floor walk-up!) apartment on Summit Court, near the Cathedral. The Fitzgeralds had lived in that same area in earlier days.

Ole Rolvaag was a young immigrant from Norway, settling in Minnesota. His book is a translation and a gripping account of the immigrant struggle in harsh, unforgiving pioneer land. An appreciated "thank you" for my driving us to the Elderhostel, from my good Norwegian friend, Barb.

Although Jon Hassler is a relative newcomer to the literary scene, our Yale Professor Emeritus was almost lavish in his praise of the author's work. The novelist received degrees from St. John's University in Minnesota, where he taught English and was writer-in-residence, and from the University of North Dakota. He has a remarkable talent for bringing his characters to life, making the reader really care for them, too. *A Green Journey*, one of his six published novels, was filmed for TV. With Angela Lansbury starring as the retired parochial school principal traveling in Ireland, it became a television treasure.

The selection of Bill Holm as the fifth "great Minnesota author" was somewhat of a surprise. As was the title of his work, *Boxelder Bug Variations*, a soft-cover book. Unknown to many of us, Bill Holm is an accomplished composer, with fingers that coax magnificent music out of a piano keyboard and other musical instruments, too.

A course in Astronomy, a subject about which my fund of knowledge was ripe for bolstering, was conducted by a young Ph.D on the University's faculty. He was bright, articulate and crystal-clear in his explanations. He considered all questions worthy of clear, understandable answers. His coup d'état was setting up telescopes on a spacious plaza for an evening class. Viewing the darkened Midwest's summer skies as he narrated information relating to the various planets was fascinating.

Generalization though it may be, elderhostelers are good conversationalists, warm and approachable. Noting the name tag on a woman in our group and her Oxford, Mississippi residence, I commented, "You're from Eudora Welty country, aren't you?" "Yes, and also from John Grisham's hometown. He and his wife are just as nice people as they were before he became a famous author." By now, three of Grisham's best-selling novels had been made into films. Testimony, we agreed, of the author's level-headedness.

One of my top-rated elderhostels was at Sheldon Jackson College in Sitka, Alaska. Tish Osada, head of the Children's section at our local library, accompanied me on the Alaska adventure. We had decided that, after the week-long Sitka program, we'd rent a station wagon for a week's further exploration. We had also accepted the enthusiastic invitation of my former Armour associate, Ruth Klumb, to stop over to visit her in her retirement home on Camano Island in the northeastern portion of Puget Sound. Ruth had been our West Coast "Marie Gifford" during the fifties and sixties and we'd worked together on many projects. Our three-day late-May stay with her, against a background of rhododendrons and azaleas everywhere—and Ruth's warm Scandinavian hospitality—was delightful. She prepared a picture-pretty Saturday afternoon tea so we could meet her neighbors, many of them Alaskan snow-birds.

James Michener, we were told, resided at Sheldon Jackson College while working on his book, *Alaska*. Sitka itself is a long, narrow strip of rain forest, a dot on the Alaska map a bit south of Juneau. Sitka at one time was Alaska's capital. It has retained much of the Russian atmosphere: minarets, towers, and architectural details commonplace in 1867 when the United States purchased Alaska from Russia. Secretary of State William Seward, who negotiated and signed the treaty, authorizing the purchase for $7.2 million, did not meet with widespread approval of that decision. The purchase became known as "Seward's Folly."

Monday's beginning class addressed what a scant deposit of North American literature exists for us to examine. Our well-informed young instructor mentioned names of several authors, which some of the men in the class recognized. Robert W. Service was certainly one of these. He's perhaps best known for The Shooting of Dan McGrew and The Cremation of Sam McGee which appear in his book, *Songs of a Sourdough*.

The second class was a look at how Russian royalty lived in Alaska before the sale to the United States. How difficult transitions were planned and implemented. Our instructor, a professor at Sheldon Jackson who was also a member of an Orthodox Church in Sitka, had prepared a fine lecture on Russian Church History for our first day of class. It provided the basis for discussion in following class sessions of the political events and the social lives of the Russian royals. One class consisted of a tour of our professor's church and a weaving together of the information she shared with us.

When Elderhostel ended on Friday, the option available to Tish and me in traveling from Sitka to Juneau was overnight ferry. Our "beds" were like airline seats or recliners. (If we'd had bed rolls, we could have slept on the upper deck, under the stars.) The ferry stopped at every little dot on the map, but we were pleasantly surprised at what a "scout's honor" code of behavior seemed to apply. Noise was minimal. Dim lights went on and off as passengers got off or on. Neither Tish nor I had any trouble sleeping, snacked at intervals and were ravenous for brunch when we reached Juneau mid-morning on Saturday. A 16-hour trip from Sitka! We were able to fit in a short boat trip to view the almost spellbinding glaciers before flying from Juneau to Anchorage.

Betty Lipstreu, niece of my Army dietitian friend, Martha Barmes, welcomed us at the airport and drove us to her apartment. As I'd asked her to do, she had made reservations for us at her Aunt Martha's favorite restaurant. We were unpacking when suddenly a distinct movement of the entire area, lasting only seconds, occurred. "Did you feel it?" Betty asked. "It was definitely a slight tremor." Over an elegant dinner, Betty unfolded her plans to take us to the Anchorage Earthquake Museum the next day. The Museum was developed after the catastrophic quake that struck south-central Alaska on Good Friday, March 27, 1964. It caused about 139 deaths and became known as the Great Alaskan or the Good Friday Earthquake. At that date it was cited as the third strongest earthquake in recorded history. We were touched by the priest's re-enactment of the service, no doubt being held that day in any number of Russian Orthodox Churches. When the quake actually hit—and lasted over 4 ½ minutes—we were not quite prepared. The persistent rumble and vibrations threatened to up-root us from our comfortable museum seats.

Betty had taught "out in the bush" but was now with the Anchorage school system, which was winding down for the school year. She proved to have the same thoughtfulness and warmth genes her Aunt Martha had. To make the most of the short time we'd have in Anchorage, she had stocked her refrigerator and cabinets with ham, turkey, beef and smoked salmon, assorted breads and rolls, as well as fresh fruits. A picnic was the plan for our second day there, giving her the chance to show us the Anchorage area. She also provided us with a Milepost Book to guide us on our trek up to Denali, on one of the only two highways in Alaska. We planned to stay in Denali for a few days, to be sure that we would be fortunate enough to view Mt. McKinley. Betty forewarned us that that may not happen. She marked the Milepost book with interesting places to stop along the way, either for their camera shots or their restroom value.

In Denali, we joined a group at 4:30 a.m. for a Wildlife Bus Tour, up through mountainous country where wildlife still reigns. That afternoon we spent with Terri, the "little neighbor" to whom I used to read and who now was a park ranger in Denali. There was nary a flake of snow heaped on the ground or floating in the air, but Terri wanted to demonstrate the skills of her favorite Huskies, beautiful dogs who must have been puzzled by grassy terrain underfoot. Then, as we were eating early supper, the grey clouds stepped aside and Mt. McKinley "came out"—and stayed in and out—in all its splendor until we returned to Anchorage the next day for our flight back to Dubuque.

Noel's retirement allowed more travel time for Mary and him. However, before long his health failed. After the feared onset of dementia and an extended period of care by Mary, transferring him to a top-rated nursing home proved to be the wisest option. Care there was consistently excellent. Mary's daily visits, the bright spots in Noel's confused, frustrating days. Medical checks revealed no imminent signs of death.

On September 28, 2004, Father Chris had reached "the Big 5-0." He delayed the traditional family celebration because of his father's situation. He had settled for a reception at the Briggitine Retreat

House in Darien, where he served the sisters as spiritual director. The reception, on Halloween Sunday was to be their birthday gift to him. Noel's unexpected death came on Tuesday, October 26th. The wake on the 28th, and the funeral on Friday, the 29th. That left Saturday for reaffirming the decision not to cancel or postpone the party. Noel would have rejoiced that we were all together honoring his first-born son's 50th birthday.

2008-2013

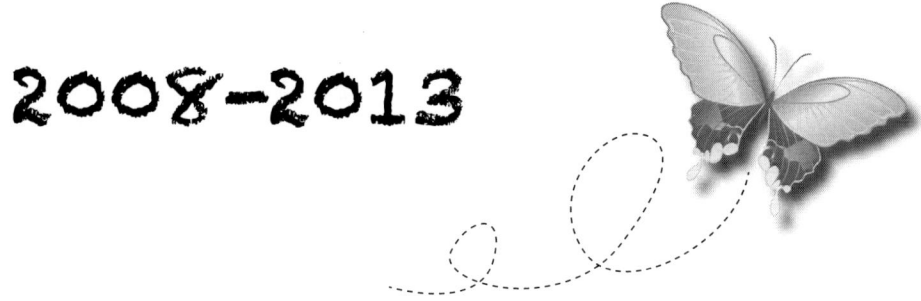

The decision to give up driving is a set-in-cement step to losing your independence—<u>unless</u> you have thoughtful family and friends who become faithful volunteer drivers. I trust that I've exercised the independence required by my career and lifestyle without too much "starchiness." In 2011 I decided to move to a retirement home. I wanted to spare my loving but dwindling family from having to make difficult decisions—for me and for themselves—later on.

A highlight of the retirement days was my participation in the Veterans' Honor Flight Program. The highly successful program provides veterans, at no cost to them, with the opportunity for inclusion in a 1-day flight from their home base into Washington, D.C. to visit the six national war memorials. Each veteran is accompanied by a "guardian" or guide.

<u>War Memorials</u>:

Lincoln Memorial
Washington Monument
World War II Memorial
Korean Memorial
Viet Nam Memorial
Arlington National Cemetery

Our flight on Monday, September 24, 2012 numbered 100 passengers, 25 of whom were World War II veterans. Of this group I happened to be the only female veteran, having served as a hospital dietitian in the U.S. Army's Women's Medical Specialist Corps. I was privileged, with Perry Mason, flight director, to place a wreath on the beautiful WW II Memorial, when our entire group visited it.

On Sunday evening before our Honor Flight an orientation dinner had been held at the Fair Grounds on the edge of town. My good friend Barb Schroeder, a retired super-active teacher, was my guardian. In truth, she had been the chief promoter of my participation from the start. Registration came first. We were each given a backpack holding a disposable camera, a pocket-size notebook for jottings along the way, a handsome *D C Photo Book, an Insider's View of Washington, D C*. The soft-cover book by Stephen R. Brown is replete with striking color photos which we would be viewing the next day. And then—we were provided with bright red T-shirts and polyester jackets bearing the message, "Honor Flight of Greater Dubuque." An effective identification device, we learned later, if several flights from various towns should be visiting the memorials at the same time. On our day there, a green-garbed group from Wisconsin was also there. We mingled but didn't mix and perhaps risk winding up on the wrong bus.

The Dubuque Honor Flight staff treated us like royalty, serving a delicious continental breakfast at Grand Harbor Hotel as we signed in. On our arrival at Dulles Airport, a welcoming group greeted us warmly, setting the tone for the entire day. There, and at many places, band music, and often bag-pipes filled the air. Wheel chairs and walkers were available if needed. Because of the time factor, and group management, from breakfast through supper, well-balanced, satisfying box lunches were served us on the plane.

Weather-wise, the day could not have been more ideal. Sunny but pleasantly cool, with fluffy white clouds cavorting about in the blue, blue sky. From memorial to memorial our group proceeded, absorbing well-researched details from our well-informed Honor Flight hosts.

After our last stop, at Arlington National Cemetery, timed to observe Changing of the Guard, it was close to suppertime. We ate our box lunches in cool, crisp air, the sun sinking fast. Then we boarded the bus to take us to the airport and were delighted when Al Bailey, the Honor Flight authority on Viet Nam, assured us that Honor Flight had not overlooked the importance of mail call to veterans. They had contacted our families and friends to write us notes, welcoming us back home. From a stack of well-filled 12 x 15 manila envelopes, he distributed one to each of us. An Honor Flight souvenir that will bring back precious memories of wartime mail call.

At the airport when Perry Mason checked for the OK to drive onto the tarmac to board our plane, he returned quickly with a not-too-happy announcement. "Our flight is being delayed. There's been a security threat." The delay was brief, thank God, and we were soon homeward-bound and pleasantly weary. Grateful for a day that was planned with such sensitivity and so well coordinated. A sincere tribute from start to finish.

The following mid-Summer another trip east followed the unforgettable Honor Flight. My sister Mary would be celebrating her 90th birthday in August. Her five adult offspring were committed to make it a real surprise bash. They had told me of their plan in early Spring. They'd schedule it in mid-July so as to squash any suspicions their Mom might have as her birthday drew near. I had pledged secrecy and circled the date on my calendar. But I did have doubts about making the trip. A recent bad fall had affected my balance, making me rely more on my cane and walker. I longed to be there—"getting there" was another story. Mary's son, Msgr. Chris, is pastor of St. Joseph's Church in suburban Shelton, about a half-hour from home. He called one evening to report that he and his siblings had had another "summit meeting" on planning the surprise. "Now, Aunt Rita, don't say anything till I tell you our plan." (I complied, trying to envision how these five independent thinkers could arrive at a plan.) "We have two airline tickets, one for you and one for whatever friend you'd like to have accompany you. Plan on staying three or four days. We'll make reservations at a nice motel not far from the church and our recently renovated pastoral center. That's where the Saturday surprise luncheon will be. You're a big part of the surprise, you know. You've got to be here!"

The pastoral persuasion was effective and I felt sure that my experienced Honor Flight Guardian, Barb, would be happy for this assignment. She had gotten to know Mary, had met several of Mary's family—and had never been to the Northeast. She knew it would be a joyous occasion. And a joyous occasion it was—a certified surprise. For a mother who has given so much and for a family who has reciprocated beyond telling. Love permeated the Center all afternoon and at Father Chris's afternoon Mass offered for his now-nonagenarian Mom.

Mary's happy entry into her nineties means that in January of 2018, God willing, her sister Rita will become a CENTENARIAN. I hope she'll be here to help celebrate!

Merci, Gracias, Danke, Tak, THANK YOU

Preparing this part of a memoir is a tricky task. By Fives to Ninety-Five almost exhausts my list of persons in this near-century of life to whom I am eternally grateful. Also, to the list of happenings, large and small, which are carved in secure memory niches.

In writing the book, I had the generous assistance of Betty Baule, a reference librarian, who had just retired from our downtown Carnegie-Stout Public Library. With several other friends, she had planned the 95th Birthday Surprise, which was a really touching gift. And which resulted in the group's insistence on my putting it all in print.

When half-way into the writing, I had announced to Betty that authorship would include her name. Did she prefer "with Elizabeth or with Betty Baule?" She was quick to reply, "No, no, no! I just want to be your amanuensis!" So, dear AMANUENSIS, a hundred thousand "thank-you's!" For your skills contribution, your reliability, your enthusiasm, your friendship.

Photo Editing by

NICC
Prepress and Printing Class

Linda Cina
Kara Porter
Jake Robertson
Instructor:
Carla Heathcote